Darlene
Hope you
the BOOK!
I was fun to recall
different facets of my
career....

Lou Bifonti '07

The Cosmic Spiderweb

How to capture *any* customer
through Event Marketing

Lou Bitonti

Dog Eat Dog Publications

Requests for permission to make copies of any part of this work should be mailed to Permissions Department, Dog Eat Dog Publications, 2555 Golf Crest Rd., Rochester Hills, MI 48309.

ISBN: 0-9749427-0-7

First Edition

Printed in the United States of America by Dog Eat Dog Publications on acid-free paper.

Table of Contents

Acknowledgments

"There is nothing more difficult to plan, more doubtful of success, no more dangerous to manage than the creation of a new system. For the initiator has the enmity of all who would profit by the preservation of the old system and merely the lukewarm defenders in those who would gain by the new one."

— Niccolò Machiavelli, *The Prince*

Why did I write this book? It's a question I continue to ask myself. Probably my business associates, friends and family have, at times, asked the same question. Sure, I have credentials, but it's not that I'm smarter than others in my field. I think the real reason is a combination of factors: I have something to say about event marketing and I've been lucky. My years with DaimlerChrysler have been in an overall sense the best I could have asked for in a career decision.

While in college and at the beginning of my career, I always knew, inside, that I looked at things a little differently than others did. I imagined and visualized different ideas, whether they were in the advertising world, the restaurant business or just life in general.

But I *did* know I harbored inside of me a lot of creativity that was ultimately allowed to emerge and express itself fully because of my career at DaimlerChrysler. Through the years, I've met, traveled and worked with some of the brightest, most humorous, most disciplined and driven people in the automotive world. Little did I know when I was in college, as I worked in auto factories during the summers to pay for tuition, that I would end up at the senior management level and be part of marketing teams that led to tremendous automotive successes—as well as troubling downtimes. It has been stated many times, "This isn't a business for the fainthearted." How true, but how exciting!

DaimlerChrysler gave me the opportunity to try ideas, execute them and measure their success . . . *or* watch them miss the mark.

Notice, I didn't use the word "failure." That's because I don't believe in it. The only failure in business—as in life—is in not taking the chance to see if an idea will work, if it can make a difference in the marketplace. There are a lot of ideas generated every day, but they are *only* ideas if they can't be implemented with creativity, sound processes and measured objectives.

I've learned and continue to learn that business ideas are only as good as the marketplace (i.e., consumers) relates or responds to them. If any idea can't be implemented into promoting a company's product or image, then you might as well go back to the drawing board and start over again. But, that's the beauty of this business; you can see a concept come to life and, if successful, make an impact. That can be very satisfying.

I've always approached business with the team concept. (No doubt, over the years many of the suppliers I worked with would probably disagree with this statement. I was never shy in stating my case, vision or direction.) But I *do* know you will never succeed without a strong team. The difference between good managers and great ones is the strength and diversity of the people they surround themselves with.

Great managers draw to their team people who could replace them at any time. They have no fear or self-doubt regarding their ability to lead and are the first to praise the team and the efforts of its individuals.

I strove to create a nervous tension on my projects but always relieved it with humor and acknowledgment. The one deciding factor in my self-proclaimed success is, simply, enthusiasm.

I love what I do and love to take on business challenges. My level of enthusiasm has not changed since the start of my career. You *know* when you have participated in one of my meetings. I may not always be right and the direction could be a little off-center, but it will be a journey. In athletics it is a known fact that talent will take you only so far, but heart will get you all the way there. Well, enthusiasm comes from the heart, and if you can't get up in the morning and want to persist in your endeavors with heartfelt exuberance, then it's time to look elsewhere.

Pretty easy stuff to say—or write. But I can only write what I've experienced and I can only draw on the chances and steps that I took in my 25 years in marketing.

My belief in the team concept extends to all the various compartments of my life, including the writing of this book. I couldn't have accomplished this project without the help and encouragement of many people.

At the top of my list, I'd like to thank my wife, Christine, and my children, Antonette, Christopher and Amanda, for always laughing at my ideas in the right spirit and for their unwavering support, not only as I wrote this book but also as I forged a career in event marketing.

As for the associates and friends who have inspired, guided, assisted, trusted and challenged me throughout my career, there are so many of them that I almost don't have enough room to list them. But you know who you are and I will always be in your debt.

An Opening Word

The Cosmic Spiderweb

Direct in its approach and comprehensive in its scope, *The Cosmic Spiderweb* is an illuminating look into one of the fastest-growing and most exciting sectors of the communications business—event marketing. Lou Bitonti brings 20 years of event experience at DaimlerChrysler, not to mention his innovative thinking and indelible spirit, to this engaging work.

Is this the kind of book where you have to somehow read between the lines for information? Hardly. It's all there in front of you. What is event marketing? When is it most effective? How are events developed, executed and measured? By answering these and dozens of other questions, Lou explains how you can promote your event with proven strategies that will maximize attendance and increase brand awareness. The book culminates with an in-depth case study of Lou's most successful brainchild—the automotive industry's benchmark ownership gathering called Camp Jeep®.

If P.T. Barnum, the consummate event marketer of the 19th century, could have named his successor, he might have selected someone like Lou. He's affable, possesses boundless energy and is never afraid to dream beyond the borders of the conventional. Even his book title is original. If, like a web, an event isn't spun together with the right vision, strategic thinking, tactical expertise and interactivity, it won't grab anything—especially your customers. *The Cosmic Spiderweb* is one book every marketing and sales professional will get caught up in!

Bill Morden
Vice Chairman, Executive Creative Director
BBDO Detroit

"The credit belongs to the man who is actually in the arena; whose face is marred by dust and sweat and blood; who strives valiantly; who errs and comes short again and again; who knows the great enthusiasms, the great devotions, and spends himself in a worthy cause; who at the best knows in the end the triumph of high achievement; and who at the worst, if he fails, at least fails while daring greatly . . ."

— Theodore Roosevelt, U. S. president

Introduction

"The test of a first-rate intelligence is the ability to hold two
opposed ideas in the mind at the same time, and still retain
the ability to function."

— F. Scott Fitzgerald, American writer

Author Lou Bitonti, ready to be master of ceremonies and auctioneer for the Jeep nationally sponsored Jeep Claybird Classic, 1997.

I was an event marketer even before I knew I was one. That's because I've always been as interested in creating and providing an experience for customers as I was in delivering a product. Sure, products are important components of the experience, and, ultimately, marketing is all about sales. But for as long as I can remember I've been *process-oriented*. Even as a high school football coach, my philosophy has always been that if you execute effectively between the goal lines, the score will take care of itself.

Of course, the conventional business wisdom holds that, to be successful in any marketing discipline, you need to be *results-oriented*. This "wisdom" suggests that *process* is for right-brain, creative types, the "soft," artistic disciplines (the ones that are typically expendable during tough economic times). When it comes to crunch time, and you really need to make those numbers, it's the no-nonsense, linear-thinking, results-oriented, left-brain analytical types who really understand what needs to be done to make a profit. So goes the conventional wisdom. But, like most rigid worldviews, the process-oriented, results-oriented duality is an oversimplification that tends to drive a wedge between two approaches that should be complementary.

Because event marketing at its best is superb creativity linked to sound business objectives, it is both process- *and* results-oriented. By definition, an event is an experience. And event marketing is all about focusing in on the lifestyle experiences of customers and integrating those experiences with buying preferences. Much of this concept is currently being codified into what's described as "experiential marketing." But, like I said, it's been my approach for as long as I can remember.

To a large extent, good event marketers are split personalities. On the one hand, they are *agitators* or "change agents." In my case, I've never been satisfied with the status quo, including how products are marketed to consumers. I've been privileged to have worked with some great people to develop and "nurture" some of the most successful marketing events ever created, but as successful as they've been, we challenged ourselves to implement continuous improvement. That's because customers and their needs change constantly as well. Their lifestyle preferences go through transitions as cultures evolve and values change. Effective event marketers, therefore, are constantly agitating for change, constantly alert for the need to modify and adapt. This is where a process orientation comes into play.

But in addition to being good agitators—good change agents— event marketers must also be effective *integrators*. They see connections that others might not see and bring things into alignment. It is this facility that allows successful event marketers to reconcile the need for constant change and adaptation with the hard realities of business strategies and objectives. It is also this ability that encourages creativity in developing events. A good event marketing professional can see relevance in a wide variety of human activities, from sports to music to pop culture to emerging technologies.

My earliest indoctrination into "experiential marketing" came as a restaurant owner in the 1970s. I had opened a restaurant called The Salt Mine in Detroit at a time when both the economy and social problems in that city combined to create a difficult commercial environment. Add to this situation the fact that the casualty rates for restaurant start-ups are notoriously high even under the best conditions, and you get some sense of how uncertain my prospects for success were. Oh, yes, by the way, I never had any experience in running a restaurant. The closest experience I had with restaurants was ordering off a menu.

What I learned very quickly was that in order to attract and retain customers, I had to provide them with not just a meal, but with a memorable experience. In this regard, I probably had an advantage because I was inexperienced in the restaurant business. My inexperience allowed me to look at things from a broader perspective. It allowed me to take chances because I didn't know any better and I didn't carry any negative baggage into the venture. Like a good integrator, I started looking beyond the obvious attraction—the menu and the daily fare we offered—to other sources of a positive experience. Sound, for example. At this time in Detroit, nobody offered entertainment for the lunch trade. I suppose the "conventional wisdom" on this point was "Who has time to listen to music during the one hectic hour they have for lunch during the typical business day?" However, I was unburdened by conventional wisdom. I thought, why not have some music with lunch? So, I brought in a jazz combo and my customers loved it. Immediately, the local press got wind of it and that started the ball rolling for more successes.

I offered other innovations as well. For example, I set up a cheese bar, but not the normal cheese bar. This cheese bar offered an array of cheese spreads with unusual ingredients like chocolate chips and vegetables. I also sold "oversize" martinis. I introduced individual size "personal" pizzas. I hosted wine tastings. I dressed my wait staff in distinctive Salt Mine T-shirts and insisted that they be outgoing, personable, "people-friendly" focused. All of this was designed to differentiate my restaurant from the competitors in Detroit. And it was designed to do that by providing an *experience*.

We also contributed to this experience through our "look." Our décor was radically different for the times. We had natural wood booths, sand-blasted bricks, brick floors, plants, and antique light fixtures and doors. This appearance contrasted dramatically with the typical downtown Detroit restaurant décor of the era, characterized by dark mahogany, red tones—in effect, very formal, stodgy atmospheres. Our restaurant was located among these world-famous dining establishments with long-standing reputations.

We were the new, young, brash upstart that didn't do things like everyone else did. We knew our competition, their strengths and weaknesses. We discovered our niche and positioned hard to our customers and the media.

Nowadays, many of our innovations are commonplace. But at the time, they represented the outpouring of my process-oriented brain as I strove to succeed.

Essentially, what I had was a passion for providing a memorable experience for my customers. And that's the key. Whether you are right-brain or left-brain-dominant, process-oriented or results-oriented, the really indispensable ingredient to being a successful event marketer is *passion*. The work is hard and it can often be frustrating, especially when things go wrong. Event marketers put in long hours and often deal with elements that are out of their control. And without passion, the work can discourage even the most talented practitioners. I decided to write this book because I have a passion for creating experiences for customers and want to "pay forward" some of my experiences to others who are currently playing in the "event" game or are considering it for the future. I hope that by connecting to others with the same passion, I can pass along some of what I've learned as an event marketer.

What you should take away from this book

Although it provides guidelines and advice on event marketing, *The Cosmic Spiderweb* is not a textbook. Nor is it strictly a "how-to" manual, even though it provides tips on a wide range of activities related to event marketing. Because it draws so heavily on my 20 years of experience in putting together thousands of events, in many ways *The Cosmic Spiderweb* is my personal acknowledgment of the talented collaborators with whom I've worked who have changed the event marketing landscape. And since the trend gives every indication of continued growth and increased sophistication, the more knowledge marketing executives have regarding event marketing's potential, the more effective they will be in getting their companies' products before the consumer.

Due to the incredible growth of event marketing, it is looking more and more attractive as a career destination. While the specialty is in its infancy as an academic discipline, the world of business has embraced event marketing. It is almost unthinkable today that a company like Microsoft, for example, would launch a new operating system without supporting that launch with an elaborate special event designed to demonstrate the "wow" factors of the new product in conjunction with creating consideration and sales. All of this means that specialists in event marketing will be much in demand in the coming years. And until academia catches up, it is up to those of us who have acquired our knowledge and experience on the job to provide the "body of knowledge" to those seeking careers in this demanding, but satisfying, field.

Perhaps most importantly, this book is also designed to appeal to the sales executive or marketing manager who is still on the fence about the value of event marketing. In today's economic world, the consumer is king. Only by inviting the consumers to participate in the marketing process can we expect them to buy with enthusiasm and trust.

I have a real-world example to illustrate this concept. As of this writing, auto manufacturers and car buyers continue to be under assault for making, purchasing and driving SUVs. (In the very week that I write these words, the popular "Doonesbury" comic strip by Garry Trudeau is in the middle of an episode wherein Mike Doonesbury's daughter is on a campaign to "ticket" SUV owners, which includes her father, and the January 12, 2004, issue of *The New Yorker* magazine contains a major article on SUVs entitled "Big and Bad.") The people who are running the various campaigns against SUVs have a variety of agendas, but one of the most compelling is safety, or, specifically, what they consider the SUV's *lack* of safety. Now, car salespersons can try a number of tactics to persuade a customer that SUVs are safe. They can cite statistics or they can refer to a vehicle's design and engineering. They can even solicit the endorsements of other SUV owners.

But nothing works like letting a prospective customer test-drive the SUV on an off-road course, "putting seats in seats" as car dealers say. And we're not just talking about your enhanced test drive on a dirt road. For the past several years, under my supervision and direction, DaimlerChrysler has sponsored events that encourage drivers to test the safety and endurance of their Jeep vehicles under extreme conditions that most drivers would never encounter in their day-to-day driving. Originally called Jeep 101 and since renamed the Route 2003 tour, this event travels to markets across the nation,

Staging area for the off-road Jeep 101 segment of the successful "Route 2003" national driving tour featuring Dodge, Chrysler and Jeep brands.

erecting "brand cities" over 30 acres, with a variety of environments, activities and test tracks for each. At these sites, customers can take Jeep vehicles across rocky surfaces, up steep hills, over potholes the size of bathtubs, and along side-hill inclines that would challenge the stability of any vehicle. The driver is accompanied by a trained "specialist" who keeps the driver informed of the dynamics of the vehicle as it tackles the road's obstacles. When the customer can experience how the vehicle performs under these conditions, all the distortion and misinformation about the safety of SUVs dissolves in the presence of the reality of the firsthand, off-road experience. This is the kind of message that traditional advertising can't deliver. Nothing can change a "comfort zone" like an experience of a product-immersion's "defining moment" that event marketing such as a Route 2003 can provide.

Jim Smith, retired Head Corporate Retail Trainer for Daimler-Chrysler, who now gives consumer orientations at events such as Route 2003, explains: "This is not a sales event. We don't have auto dealers on-site. What

Off-roading staging for over 2,000 jeeps at Camp Jeep, 2002.

Winching demonstrations on Jeep Wrangler capabilities at Camp Jeep, 2000.

we would like the customer to do is to say, 'This driving experience has opened my eyes. I will go to a Chrysler, Dodge or Jeep dealership with more product information and an enhanced comfort zone in making my purchase decision.'"

For a "people person" like myself, I can think of no more rewarding career than that of event marketing manager. The "up-close-and-personal" opportunity to interact with customers as human beings during an event rather than as part of a "target audience" or a "demographic" is unique in the marketing field. Talk about instant gratification! Experiencing a customer's excitement as he or she encounters your product not on a shelf or in a showroom, but as an extension of his or her daily life, is one of the most satisfying rewards that any marketing executive can realize. I hope that, if nothing else, you can take that away with you after reading this book.

Chapter 1
The Event Marketing Experience

"Put your heart, mind, and soul into even your smallest acts. That is the secret of success."

— Swami Sivananda, 20th century religious teacher

The Cosmic Spiderweb

. . . We were doing "Jeep Superstars" on ABC and the episode was being filmed in Mexico. We had all the camera crew, judges, athletes and celebrities waiting on location. However, we had a slight problem . . . we couldn't get the Jeeps across the border. The only way we were going to get those vehicles across was for me to drive to the border and meet with the Mexican border officials to give them cash so they would let the vehicles in the country. Without doing that, I would have had no vehicles and no show . . .

. . . We're doing Spring Break in Daytona Beach in the late 80s. I'd never done one before and I didn't know what to expect. We had built a sand dune out on the beach to display the new Plymouth Laser, which was the new concept car at the time. Now, concept cars can be worth up to half a million dollars. I go to bed that night on the 15th floor of the hotel, and at 4:00 a.m. I'm awakened by this pounding on my veranda door. I open the curtains to find that a hurricane is coming through and the pounding is my inflatable balloon we were using as part of the display, which has come loose from its moorings and is pounding against my balcony a couple hundred feet above the beach. Next thing I see are my corporate banners flying around, and through the havoc I

look down to the beach to see that the wind and water have blown the sand away from under the concept car, which is now supported only by a flimsy metal structure we had used to build the sand mound and display the vehicle. And I realize at that moment that half a million dollars was about to go floating out into the ocean . . .

. . . It was the opening day of Camp Jeep. We had just gone through 16 days of rain and the ground was so wet that we had to put down our own gravel road so that the trucks wouldn't sink as we unloaded displays. But opening day was bright and sunny. I had done my annual walk-through the previous day, and all the displays, exhibits and activity areas appeared to be in order. Nevertheless, just before the crowds started to arrive, I was doing one more tour of the grounds. I especially had one area I wanted to inspect. Along with the Callaway golf people, we had set up a phenomenal golf academy at the event. We had erected a huge tent that would have rivaled any pro shop. It housed six golf pros and 12 swing cages, not to mention the golf equipment itself. The reigning long-ball champ was scheduled to join us to do demonstrations, so we had a bleacher section. We also had putting greens and sand traps set up. It was gorgeous. So, I figured, here was a chance for me to hit a few balls before all the guests arrived and things got too busy. I asked for a bucket of balls—only to learn that there were none around. It was the opening day of the event; six thousand people were about to arrive, and this promised to be one of the top attractions at Camp Jeep. And I had no golf balls . . .

Welcome to the world of event marketing, where the unexpected is expected.

Any book that calls itself *The Cosmic Spiderweb* has some explaining to do, first of all, about that title. This is, after all, a book on event marketing, not a spacey treatise on some mystical, galactic force of nature. What does a spiderweb, a cosmic one, no less, have to do with event marketing? Better yet, what exactly is event marketing? Dan Hanover, editorial director at *Event Marketer* magazine, defines event marketing as follows: "A face-to-face connection between a company and a customer or consumer, taking place in a live setting using at least three of the five senses." It's a definition I can agree with as far as it goes. What's conspicuous by its absence in this definition is any mention of a sale or transaction. That's because, in event marketing, the priority is on the *experience*—whatever transpires during that phenomenon that *Event Marketer* magazine's use of the term "connection" refers to. Notice also the premium on the *senses*. As we'll see, event marketing is all about customers' emotional experiences of products, and the senses are the gateways to the emotions. If I were to add anything to this definition, it would be the word "memorable" as in a "*memorable* face-to-face connection between a company and a customer or consumer." As we shall see, the memorability of an experience is what gives it meaning and continuity. But this is a minor quibble.

Let's get back to the spiderweb image. As it turns out, the cosmic spiderweb has a lot to do with event marketing. Earlier in my marketing career my colleagues and I found the term useful for envisioning the vast unifying structure behind the apparent chaos of event marketing planning and implementation. Sometimes with an amused outlook, and at other times with a stressful grin, we would start asking ourselves, "Can you see the cosmic spiderweb taking shape?"

The cosmic spiderweb is an apt metaphor for what has become one of the fastest growing and most significant marketing trends of the past decade. As *Event Marketer* magazine observed in an article on DaimlerChrysler's experience in event marketing, mainstream advertising has taken a back seat to "fully blown, elaborately produced live events—where the touch, feel, smell and the sound of glass, rubber, steel and leather put the consumer into 'up-close-and-personal contact with the object of his desire.'"

A presentation by the Promotion Marketing Association's recently formed Event Marketing Council underscored the amazing growth of event marketing by reporting some impressive budgetary trends. For example, citing a 2002 study by Intellitrends, a Michigan-based research organization, the Council noted that "47 percent of companies feel that event marketing provides the 'greatest return on investment' when compared to other marketing and communications tactics—advertising, direct mail, sales promotion, Internet, etc." In addition:

- 38 percent of companies anticipated higher budget allocations for event marketing.

- Among automotive, technology, media/entertainment, consumer electronics and healthcare industries, budget allocations were expected to rise 23 percent.

- More than 22 percent of the total marketing budget is now earmarked for events, "a number that is consistent regardless of industry."

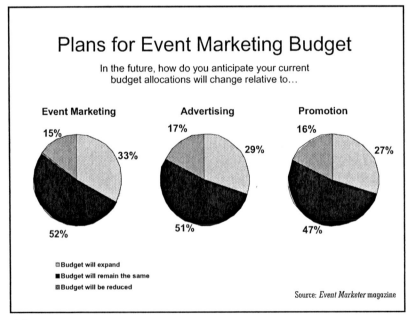

Plans for Event Marketing Budget

In the future, how do you anticipate your current budget allocations will change relative to…

Event Marketing
15%
33%
52%

Advertising
17%
29%
51%

Promotion
16%
27%
47%

▩ Budget will expand
■ Budget will remain the same
▣ Budget will be reduced

Source: *Event Marketer* magazine

The Cosmic Spiderweb

The image of the cosmic spiderweb perfectly captures the complexity, variety and yet the interconnectedness of the various components that come together—often, it *seems,* as effortlessly as a spider spins its web—to create the contemporary special event. Of course, it is not effortless at all. The hard work of many talented experts goes into every one of the thousands of events held each year in the United States and throughout the world. (According to independent market analyst Datamonitor, event marketing spending recently rose at a compound annual growth rate of 9.5 percent in Europe, underscoring the fact that the phenomenon is not limited to America.) Indeed, much of what is contained in this book describes the various roles and responsibilities of the team members critical to staging an effective event. Perhaps that is one way in which the spiderweb analogy falters. The spider may work its web magic through solitary effort, but event marketing is the ultimate *team* endeavor. It is an active, dynamic and, most important, *collaborative* process that appears seamless when it's done right.

Another reason the spiderweb comparison is so appropriate is the "capture" motif of my subtitle. As beautiful as the spiderweb is in its intricacy of engineering, it's important to keep in mind that the spider doesn't engage in this activity simply to decorate its surroundings. The spiderweb has an overriding practical purpose—to acquire food. Likewise, notwithstanding the power of the special event to excite the senses, the ultimate objective of modern marketing events is to sell products. We are capturing customers, just as the spider captures flies. Of course, our "captive audience" is detained by their own consent, a consent they are willing to offer depending on the event marketer's ability to "capture" their imaginations.

Whatever symbol we use to express the essence of event marketing, the discipline has definitely come of age. Whereas in the past, special events may have played a *supporting* role in the marketing mix—primarily by increasing product awareness—event marketing is now fully integrated into the overall marketing strategy. And these are not just "shows." The focus of marketing events today is on personal interaction—opportunities for customers to bond with products and the people who sell them.

The Strengths of Event Marketing

The 2003 Event Trends survey conducted by George P. Johnson Co. and co-sponsored by *Event Marketer* magazine and Meeting Professionals International (MPI) provides some insight on the growth of event marketing. The study states that in 2002 there were more than 12,000 trade shows in North America and that more than a million event-scale meetings were held at an investment of approximately $100 billion. *PROMO* magazine, in a study co-sponsored with the Promotion Marketing Association (PMA) called "The 2003 Trends Report," reported that 56 percent, or $132 billion, of the total $233.7 billion spent in 2002 in consumer promotions was devoted to event marketing. That was an increase of six percent from 24 percent in 2001 to 30 percent in 2002. That's a significant commitment and testifies to the importance the discipline has assumed.

And the enthusiasm for event marketing shows no signs of slowing down. In its 2002 Corporate Event Marketplace study, *Special Events* magazine found that 70 percent of respondents said they planned to stage the same number of events in 2003 as they do in a typical year. And 28 percent were planning to hold an even greater number of events.

Why has event marketing grown into such a powerful marketing force in recent years? To answer this question, it is important to recognize that the growth of event marketing reflects the evolution of some of the cultural values in our society. One of the key words describing that cultural evolution is *entertainment*. Technology and affluence have combined to create a culture that demands gratification of the senses. And today, we don't want to be passive consumers of entertainment. Nowadays, *interactivity* is the key factor in entertainment. Even traditionally passive forms of entertainment such as movies have elbowed their way into the interactive realm by marketing DVDs that allow a much richer—and more optional—viewing experience, including alternative endings. (Not everybody thinks of this trend as an advance. Terrence Rafferty in the *New York Times Magazine*, lamented the alternative endings available on many DVDs of Hollywood films. "All I'm saying, really," he writes, "is that watching a film is, and should be, an experience different from that of playing Myst or placing an order on Amazon." Notwithstanding his objection, interactivity rules.) Of course, interactivity has long been the hallmark of video games, sports fantasy camps and theme parks. Today, for example, if you want to go beyond the passive consumption of the Spider-Man movie adventure, you can skip the movie and, instead, head for the spectacular "Adventures of Spider-Man" ride at the Universal Studios Florida theme park in Orlando, where you literally become part of the action.

(In fact, we've come full circle on this. The release of Disney's *Pirates of the Caribbean: The Curse of the Black Pearl* derives from the theme park show of the same name in Disney World, the ultimate event venue. The theme park show was enjoyed by millions and now it has been reconnected again through the movie.)

This trend toward the "participatory audience" has only in the last decade or so been leveraged as a marketing asset, and it has happened most spectacularly in the environment of the special event. With the lines between entertainment and enticement blurred, customers now demand a more immediate, experiential relationship with the products they are being induced to purchase, whether it's a virtual walk-through of a home still in the blueprint stage, the enhanced "test drive" on a real race track or off-road course, or just the opportunity to shake hands with a celebrity spokesperson. And this three-dimensional, experiential relationship is what the event marketing provides in a "spontaneous" and live arena.

It is a way of connecting products with lifestyle that creates the "Camp Jeep phenomenon," for example, wherein, every year, brand and prod-

"There's a reason it's called event marketing."

If there is a most important thing to remember about event marketing, it's that the principles apply irrespective of the event's size and complexity. Objectives still have to be identified, metrics still need to be determined and the activities of the event need to serve the higher purpose of creating visibility, buzz and, eventually, sales. Without these elements, you might have a nice time, but you're not likely to provide an enriching experience for your customers.

uct loyalty become a way of life—a cultural value. How else do you account for the fact that 8,000 Jeep owners were willing to pay almost $300 per vehicle to attend "Camp Jeep" in 2003 in Charlottesville, Virginia, and have done so annually for nearly a decade?

Another great strength of event marketing is that, as an integral part of the marketing mix, it also encompasses other traditional marketing disciplines such as advertising and public relations. In doing so, it magnifies and intensifies the appeal to consumers' needs and desires, turbo charging this appeal, basically, to increase sales. Because events are often, by definition, newsworthy activities, event marketing works particularly well with public relations, which can bring to bear its formidable media relations capabilities to enhance an event's prestige and effectiveness through third-party recognition and credibility. Additionally, event marketing reaches out to consumers cost effectively.

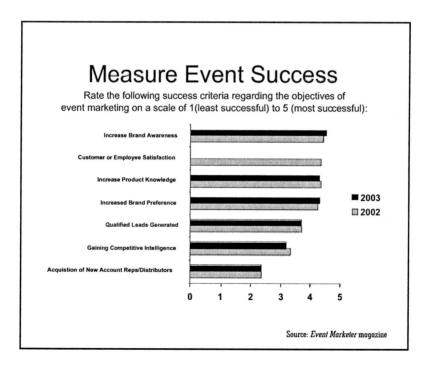

Measure Event Success

Rate the following success criteria regarding the objectives of event marketing on a scale of 1(least successful) to 5 (most successful):

Increase Brand Awareness
Customer or Employee Satisfaction
Increase Product Knowledge
Increased Brand Preference
Qualified Leads Generated
Gaining Competitive Intelligence
Acquistion of New Account Reps/Distributors

■ 2003
▨ 2002

0 1 2 3 4 5

Source: *Event Marketer* magazine

And when it comes to the Holy Grail of marketing—Return on Investment—event marketing has a clear advantage over other components of the marketing mix. I'll expand upon this advantage in a later chapter in this book, but suffice it to say for now that when you literally have your customers in sight, when you can judge with your own eyes their responses to your products and messages, it is easier to get a sense of the effectiveness of those messages and the appeal of your products. It's all about getting close to the customer.

Finally, I've been discussing event marketing in the sense of the mammoth extravaganzas that often run into the millions of dollars to produce. The reality is that most businesses don't have the budgets to support those kinds of programs. But the beauty of event marketing is that it works on a small as well as a large scale. The fundamental principles and rules apply whether your budget is $1,000 or $1 million.

Having said all this, it's important to acknowledge that event marketing hasn't eclipsed other marketing methods to the point that they've become irrelevant. TV advertising, public relations, direct mail and other marketing communications approaches remain vital and important parts of the mix. In fact, as we'll see later in this book, event marketing isn't always the appropriate marketing choice. Events must align with marketing strategy; cost effectiveness must be considered. Events cannot be just "social functions"—they must serve a business purpose.

Nevertheless, the powerful emotional connection that can be made between the consumer and the product in the environment of event marketing is revolutionizing the transactional dynamic. As Marc Gobé, president, chief executive officer and creative director of d/g* worldwide writes in *Emotional Branding*, " . . . understanding people's emotional needs and desires is really, now more than ever, the key to success. Corporations must take definite steps toward building stronger connections and relationships which recognize their customers as partners. Industry today needs to bring people the products they desire, exactly when they want them, through venues that are both inspiring and intimately responsive to their needs." Gobé is discussing emotional branding, but the inspiring and intimately responsive venues he refers to perfectly describe the opportunity presented by event marketing.

Event marketing's role in retaining customer loyalty

Event marketing can attract new customers to products, but the discipline is particularly effective in promoting customer loyalty. To the marketers of products and services, the desirability of customer loyalty seems intuitive and obvious. But it goes beyond the concept of mere repeat sales.

Loyal customers are repeat purchasers, but that is just the beginning of their contribution to profitability. Loyal customers are less price-sensitive, allowing a company to sustain higher margins. Loyal customers are more prone to purchase products from an expanded brand lineup, meaning that they

Jeep historical tent at Camp Jeep depicting the long and storied history of Jeep vehicle lineage.

allow you to expand your market within your current customer base. Loyal customers spread the word about their experiences to family and friends, bringing in other customers who also are prone to loyalty because they already are connected to the brand through social relationships. Loyal customers are easier and cheaper to reach with marketing messages, and they are more responsive to them. Finally, loyal customers are more forgiving of your mistakes.

Event marketing can enhance customer loyalty because, as a marketing approach, it forms the most intimate bond with customers. It appeals to what animates the passions of customers by focusing on lifestyle preferences. Ideally, it closely tracks opinions and attitudes through on-site measurement. Event marketing can also provide an emotional experience of community with customers who share common interests. And event marketing allows a relationship between the customer and the product that is participatory. Customers contribute to the product's ongoing development. They become an integral part of the process rather than mere "end-users."

Other thoughts on the strengths of event marketing

• **Event marketing doesn't *impose*; it *invites*.** Traditional advertising can be seen as intrusive, even though the intrusion may be passive. A display ad in a newspaper, for example, intrudes itself on the editorial content of the paper and, in so doing, becomes an impediment to our reading of the paper. Of course, we've become so accustomed to this particular form of intrusion that we often don't even resent it. In fact, much to the chagrin of advertisers, we often don't even notice these ads anymore. Clearly, a more obvious intrusion in our lives is the television commercial, which is designed to interrupt the narrative flow of television programming, whether that narrative is a drama, a sitcom, a news show or a sporting event. We may find these interruptions more frustrating than display ads, but, again, we've grudgingly come to accept them. And, again, the irony is that commercial time on TV is the time for raids on the refrigerator and trips to the bathroom. At the most obnoxious extreme, we find the telemarketer's call, an intrusion that's almost universally resented and avoided. As Seth Godin points out in his book *Free Prize Inside: The Next Big Marketing Idea*, "What we've learned is this: In an era of too much noise and too much clutter and too many choices and too many channels and too much spam, you can't make a good living by interrupting people over and over." In contrast, event marketing makes itself available to the audience without interrupting our activities. We *choose* to include it in our schedules, and that's a big difference. It gives the consumer a measure of control, predisposing him or her to a more relaxed experience of the product.

• **Event marketing creates *experiences* rather than *hits*.** Traditional advertising is all about impressions and frequency. The assumption is that if enough people hear a marketing message often enough, sales will result. There may have been a time when this calculation worked, but it doesn't today. As I've already suggested, today's advertising must engage consumers *emotionally*. Consumers are bored, skeptical—even cynical—when it comes to advertising. They don't want to think that their response to a product is a matter of brainwashing. For the younger generation, especially, marketers need to develop "street cred," the sense that they have earned the attention of their customers. And you don't earn that attention through a constant barrage of messages that amounts to an assault on our collective consciousness. Consumers want to make up their own minds, and they want to do it by *experiencing* the product in its element, so to speak.

• **Event marketing goes beyond *awareness* to *connection*.** This point is closely aligned to the previous one, but with a subtle distinction. These days, the best that traditional one-way advertising can *hope* for is that the target audience will attain or retain an awareness of the product being advertised. Well, it can hope for more than that, but it's not likely to happen. As Al and Laura Ries point out in *The Fall of Advertising & the Rise of PR*, advertising's main function is—or should be—brand maintenance. Not building a brand, not even stimulating brand loyalty. Those functions are best left to other disciplines, namely PR and event marketing. The reason event marketing is so effective in generating the kind of enthusiasm for a brand that results in sales is that it engages the customer on a personal and emotional level in a way that mass market advertising can't. Event marketing connects consumers to products through the richness and memorability of experience, whereas advertising is limited to message without the context of experience.

• **Event marketing is *immediate* rather than *mediated.*** In the event marketing arena, customers encounter products in a direct, unfiltered way. The exposure to the product isn't dictated by the length of a TV spot or the area available on the print page. In addition, when part of a marketing event, the product is not subject to the interpretation, creative or otherwise, of the developers of the ad. Consumers are therefore free to experience the product in a context that is more meaningful to them. Embedding a product in an information medium such as a newspaper or a TV show cannot help but distort the perception of the product. That's because most ads attempt to make positive associations in presenting products. That's all well and good, but it's not necessarily an accurate representation. But at an event, the consumer's hands-on experience of the product cuts through the pretensions of advertising.

• **Event marketing is *relevant* rather than *incidental.*** Let's face it. The way most of us experience advertising is a matter of hit-and-miss. If we happen to be reading a magazine or watching a TV show or listening to the radio when a specific ad for, say, exercise equipment, appears, then maybe we'll see or hear it. Maybe we'll even read it or observe it or listen to it carefully enough for it to make a significant impression. But most of us aren't reading magazines or watching TV or listening to the radio for the ads. The ads in these various media are extraneous to our primary intention—which is to read the stories in the magazine and watch or listen to the programming on TV and radio. In other words, ads are incidental to our experience and, as such, we treat them with less attention, less concentration. The case with event marketing is much different. Because event marketers—if they are doing their jobs correctly—attract consumers with specific lifestyle preferences for which their products have affinities, a built-in relevance is already established. Hence, people who are fitness-oriented, for example, and who attend a health and fitness show where your exercise equipment is not only displayed on-site but available for use by attendees, find your approach much more relevant to their lives.

• **Event marketing offers a *dialog*, rather than a *monolog*.** With traditional advertising, the communication is one way. Of course, the consumer can react to the ad by buying the product (or by expressing frustration, anger, delight, etc., in the creative). Still, this doesn't constitute a meaningful exchange with the consumer. Events, on the other hand, offer a superb opportunity for this type of exchange. In fact, most successful events don't focus on sales at all. They focus on the experience for the customer, and a critical component in that experience is *feedback*. Some of the more popular activities at Camp Jeep every year, for example, are the engineering roundtables, which allow Jeep owners to meet with engineers to discuss issues of vehicle performance and design. Not only does this make the customer feel that his or her input is important, but it also supplies valuable data for the development of new models and the improvement of existing ones.

• **Event marketing is *customer-focused* rather than *product-focused*.** Almost by definition, traditional advertising zeroes in on the product. It is the primary reason for the ad's existence. Of course, an audience is involved, passively, in a more or less targeted way. But the audience is never engaged with traditional advertising to the extent that it is in event marketing. With event marketing, the priority is always on the customer's experience of the product, rather than simply on the product's appeal to the customer. Think of the difference between watching a TV spot for a Jeep and spending a day at Camp Jeep, where you can actually drive the car on a thrilling off-road track. And not only that. You can experience all of the associated activities that create a rich, emotional context—the cosmic spiderweb—for your enjoyment of the test drive. One approach is all about the car. The other is all about the customer. The premise of *this* book is that the customer-focused approach is the more effective approach.

Business-to-business event marketing

I've been discussing event marketing so far in the context of consumer marketing. However, event marketing is fast becoming a more important method of creating experiences for business-to-business clients, too. Unlike consumers, business-to-business customers—typically organizations or businesses themselves—usually purchase products and services not specifically as end users, but to use those products and services to generate other products or to re-sell them to other organizations.

While there are many commonalities when it comes to marketing products to consumers and businesses, there are also some differences. Just in terms of sheer numbers, the target audience among business-to-business customers is usually smaller than the target audience among consumer audiences. If you're selling automobiles, for example, you may target thousands of individual drivers among a large universe of automobile consumers, but the number may be much smaller among business-to-business clients—perhaps dozens of buyers who make decisions about organizations' fleets. On the other hand, that small number of fleet buyers is, collectively, going to buy a greater number of vehicles than any one consumer is likely to buy in a lifetime, which often increases the transaction value.

Business-to-business target audiences are also easier to identify than consumers because their function—such as the fleet buyer—defines their targetability. Business-to-business audiences usually have a higher level of expertise in the product, as well.

On the downside, when it comes to purchasing, the decision-making process is usually longer for business-to-business clients than for consumers, who typically have fewer people to answer to and fewer bureaucratic hoops to jump through.

The most recognizable business-to-business event marketing prototype is the trade show, an exhibition of industry-specific products and services. The annual Society of Automotive Engineers (SAE) World Congress is an example of this kind of trade show, which attracts industry experts as opposed to the general public. Unfortunately, many trade shows are experiencing more and more clutter these days, as many companies jockey for position to get their products and services in front of their shared customers. Event marketing offers an alternative whereby a company can enjoy a level of "exclusivity" with regard to its positioning before the customer. A good example of how this can work is provided in the following case study. I'm grateful to Jan Katzoff, CEO of SportsMark, for providing it.

Case Study: Yahoo!: Global Positioning Through a World Cup Connection

The Challenge

A first-time World Cup sponsor, Yahoo!, the popular Internet service provider, wanted to create an identity and association with this popular global sporting event. Specifically, they wanted to maximize their brand exposure and reach at World Cup events and connect the Yahoo! brand and image more closely to Internet users at the 2002 FIFA World Cup co-hosted by Korea and Japan.

The Solution

To achieve this identity and help spread the Yahoo! spirit and brand image, SportsMark, an event management and strategic marketing firm based in San Francisco, was chosen to design and implement hospitality events with Yahoo!'s corporate branding message in mind. In order to support their association with World Cup, SportsMark helped Yahoo! incorporate the Yahoo! colors and brand image with that of the Federation Internationale de Football Association (FIFA) World Cup logo. This look was then incorporated into all guest communications, both on-line and in print, as well as into on-site brand presence, including directional signage and event décor.

Hospitality Suite

This important space was considered the focal point and main gathering place for corporate guests. Yahoo! used program signage and colors, the Yahoo! corporate image and their association with World Cup in a subtle and aesthetically pleasing manner to tie the company's overall program look to this focal point. A small lounge was created around televisions and featured comfortable Japanese-style sofas and chairs, providing a relaxing environment in which to experience some of the host country's cultural essence with a Yahoo! branded design. For dining, the Yahoo! image came to life with a large buffet filled with a whimsical centerpiece of silk flowers, colored Japanese papers and Yahoo! toys.

In addition to the lounge and dining area, there was a Yahoo!-inspired Internet café where guests could actually use and experience Yahoo!'s product, thereby providing a means of personal involvement with the brand.

Welcome Reception

This event, which was designed to welcome guests to World Cup and its host countries, also worked to reinforce the association with Yahoo! and World Cup. The color scheme, again, was all Yahoo!, but with a twist. Instead of the bright purple and gold corporate colors, the event used soft purple and maize as its backdrop. To help promote the global association, the rest of the theming followed with Japanese paper centerpieces and a menu complete with flavors from Korea and Japan. After guests dined on regional cuisine, they were entertained by traditional Taiko drummers. Akebono, world champion sumo wrestler, and Miss Japan welcomed guests and stayed for a photo opportunity, which resulted in a long-lasting, tangible takeaway from this exciting event.

Semi-final Pre-game Party

Since the program's ultimate attraction was soccer/football, SportsMark decided to capitalize on the connection between the sport and Yahoo! The event's theme presented the sport with a Yahoo! flair, including a buffet filled with "game day" food and topped with a centerpiece of Yahoo! soccer balls and Yahoo! colors. Seating tables were also festive and resembled a soccer ball topped with balloons. The entertainment helped to build excitement for the upcoming match, while providing a fun way for guests to mingle by playing soccer/football-related games. The event was a casual, exciting, interactive way to entertain attendees before taking them to the semifinal match from Japan.

"See and Be Seen" Gala Reception

The initial guest invitation to the World Cup program said "the whole world will be watching," and these guests had the privilege of actually being there! That prompted the "See and Be Seen" theme, as SportsMark designed an event that all of the guests would want to be seen attending. They needed to feel as though they were invited to the hottest, most sought-after party in town, and only Yahoo! could take them there. SportsMark needed to carry out the Yahoo! look and feel, but it needed to be different from other events their guests had attended.

Guests entered a restaurant that was transformed into a hip club under a purple and yellow awning. The place was lit to create an inviting ambience, and even the welcome cocktails had a sparkling "ice" cube. Guests were videoed during the evening's festivities and their images were projected onto large screens throughout the space. They could also be "seen" at a modeling photo shoot that took place on location. A fashion photographer and models contributed to the video, and each guest received a Yahoo! souvenir photo.

The food featured the latest in menu trends with simple, updated flavors. Dancing began and it was truly the "hip" bar it was designed to be. Specialty-themed lighting enhanced the entire space, and a DJ and professional "slinky" dressed dancers built excitement on the dance floor.

Final Game

Excitement for the final match was everywhere. The pregame event was designed to build on what was already happening around Tokyo (and the rest of the world), but to give it a different twist, again, reminding guests that only Yahoo! could bring the excitement of this global sporting event to them. The event took place in a bowling alley, so, naturally, guests participated in the bowling tournament before the big match. Face painters were on hand to decorate attendees with team colors and designs. The space consisted of purple-and-yellow tables and chairs and centerpieces made of small soccer balls that represented participating World Cup countries. There was even a Yahoo! blimp flying through the event. After the game, the event continued with the same Yahoo! feel, but with an evening twist. A city lights backdrop lit the areas with the Yahoo! logo, and dancing started on the LED floor. The main feature on the dance floor was a giant soccer ball. Guests celebrated with dancing, evening glitter and dinner, and rejoiced in the postgame exhilaration brought to them exclusively by Yahoo!

The hallmarks of an effective marketing event are all here: thematic unity, interactivity, the emotional connection, the emphasis on experience rather than sales, and the customer-centric approach. As we will see throughout this book in presenting various case studies, the successful event marketer relies on these principles to make events memorable.

So, that's where we are today with event marketing. But how did we get here? What were some of the precedents and influences that led to event marketing's rapid growth and its current impact? We'll look at some of the key forces in the next chapter.

SPONSORSHIP TRENDS IN THE U.S.

➤ Migrations away from "traditional" sports packages (i.e. baseball, football, basketball, hockey) into "non-traditional" sponsorships (i.e. the arts, cultural events, theater, environmental organizations, lifestyle sports).

➤ Migrations toward cross promotions.

➤ Integration of the sponsorship through leveraging the elements of an "intelligent marketing mix" — advertising, public relations, themed graphics, and sales promotions.

➤ Enhanced on-site programs with extensions into off-site promotions. Sponsors are commercializing their association with the event prior to the event taking place. They are spending $2 to $3 on promotion for each dollar of sponsorship.

WHY CUTTING EDGE CORPORATIONS CHOOSE EVENT MARKETING

➤ Increased brand and company awareness to specific target audiences.

➤ Identification of brands with a particular active, educated lifestyle in mind.

➤ Differentiation of products from field of competitors.

➤ Opportunities for corporations to "position" themselves within a broader range of culturally diverse markets, community activities, gender.

➤ Development of select strategic, co-sponsor relationships.

➤ Penetration of and direct influence on target audience.

➤ Shape and/or reinforce the public's perception of a specific product's or brand's attributes.

➤ Create "exit barriers" for their respective brands and keep consumers from "jumping" to competitors.

Chapter Checklist

Checklist

- The "cosmic spiderweb" image captures the complexity, variety and interconnectedness of the various components that, together, create the contemporary special event.

- Event marketing is about creating an emotional and memorable face-to-face experience with the product for the customer.

- Surveys indicate that event marketing is assuming greater significance and impact when compared to more traditional forms of marketing.

- Event marketing is especially effective in developing and promoting customer loyalty.

- Return on investment—a key component in any marketing approach—can be calculated very effectively in event marketing.

Chapter 2
A Short History of Event Marketing

"Every memorable act in the history of the world is a triumph of enthusiasm. Nothing great was ever achieved without it because it gives any challenge or any occupation, no matter how frightening or difficult, a new meaning. Without enthusiasm you are doomed to a life of mediocrity, but with it you can accomplish miracles."

— Og Mandino,
American motivational author, speaker

The Cosmic Spiderweb

Archeology tells us that "special" events have been around as long as humans have been walking upright. As a social species, we have always used rituals and ceremonies to achieve objectives, whether it was to petition the heavens for a successful harvest, seek the favor of the gods in battle or to institutionalize and commemorate the key milestones of life—birth, coming of age, marriage, death and other rites of passage. Across cultures, we are conditioned to celebrate significant events collectively. In this context, the Christmas holiday season can be seen as one long (and getting longer all the time) special event.

Events have been staged to create support for political causes (and keep the populace in line) at least since the time of the games in the Roman Coliseum. They have been used to generate their own income, as was the case with P. T. Barnum's exhibitions. They have also been used, generally speaking, to create awareness for new products. The New York World's Fair in 1939 and similar subsequent expositions have served to showcase new technologies—creating advance demand for future products. However, these were primarily *spectator* events. Consumers of these events participated only passively, and the connection between the product and the consumer was relatively soft.

41

In terms of the "creators" of the discipline, commentators have identified a number of candidates as "pioneers" of the event marketing movement, including P.T. Barnum and the Ringling Brothers, baseball executive Bill Veeck, and, of course, Walt Disney. And antecedents for event marketing can be found in everything from political conventions to county and state fairs. While we should acknowledge event marketing's debt to these sources, today's event marketing is qualitatively different from the shows (and "showmanship") of the past.

Only in the last couple of decades has the concept of event marketing crystallized beyond the "hospitality event" into the dynamic, *experiential* marketing opportunity it is today. A good example is provided by the annual motorcycle pilgrimage to Sturgis, South Dakota, now in its seventh decade. Started as a get-together for nine racers of the Jackpine Gypsies Motorcycle Club, the Sturgis Rally now welcomes thousands of motorcycle enthusiasts, and hosts events ranging from races to beauty contests. It's no coincidence that companies like Harley-Davidson have a major presence at Sturgis.

Several factors have contributed to the evolution from "show" to "participation," most of them having to do with changes in consumer expectations. Let's take a brief look at some of these factors.

The growth of the entertainment industry

It is obvious to our generation that entertainment has been commercialized and vice-versa. But it wasn't always this way. While entertainment has long been a for-profit enterprise, its connection to the world of products and services wasn't always so obvious. This began to change dramatically with the introduction of the electronic mass media, and especially with the advent of television. The integration in one powerful medium of entertainment and the commercial advertising that supported it had profound effects on our consciousness, not least of which was the growing expectation that entertainment was a valid part of the everyday human experience. We also got more comfortable with the intermingling of entertainment and products, and that helped condition us to accept the commercial sponsorship of everything from rock concerts to motorcycle rallies.

In this way, commercial products have become part of our value system. We invite products into our intimate, everyday experience and, to some extent, this leads not only to brand loyalties but also to a sense of propriety over the brands that, in the past, belonged only to the manufacturers. Now, we, the consumers, want to have a say. And the event marketing experience offers the perfect environment for this kind of interchange.

And, as I've already mentioned, entertainment is no longer passive. From the virtual reality of video games to extreme sports to eco-tour vacations, the emphasis now is on participation. Nike, for example, doesn't just make commercials with sports celebrities for couch potatoes to ignore. The company sponsors 10K Fun Runs to develop and nurture customer loyalties, encourage feedback and dialog on products, and recruit consumers to promote and sell their running shoes for them.

The evolution of professional sports

In terms of direct participation, professional sports require a level of talent and skill that excludes the vast majority of humanity. As a result, for years, professional sports contests—as well as high-level collegiate sporting events—were perceived as strictly spectator sports. Of course, to a large degree, this is still true, the Walter Mitty-like fantasies of millions of weekend athletes notwithstanding. With their potential to attract large audiences, especially TV audiences, professional sports also attracted sponsorships by companies wanting to talk to these huge audiences by exposing their products to them. Still, people watched these games rather than participating in them. But that didn't mean that spectators didn't have a sense of ownership, hence loyalty, when it

Gabrielle Reese, professional volleyball player and model, conducting clinics at Camp Jeep, 2000.

came to the sports they preferred to watch. As a measure of this loyalty, consumer sales of professional athletic team wearables are at an all-time high. The Detroit Red Wings "flying wheel" logo can be seen on the apparel of fans coast-to-coast in one of the more visible statements of fan loyalty.

But even the loyalty of Red Wing fans is eclipsed by the devotion of NASCAR enthusiasts, for whom brand loyalty is off the map. The creators of NASCAR understood early on that sponsorships were essential to the survival of their sport. That also goes for fans. They are all part of one big family. Where else would you find a middle-age man walking around with a "Tide" T-shirt on? The point is, if Tide sponsors his favorite car and driver, you can almost bet he uses the product and is proud of it. If a NASCAR fan is wearing a Pennzoil hat, he or she is almost certain to be using the product in his or her own car.

In the last decade, professional sports have become more "democratized." Activities that in the past wouldn't even have counted as proper "sports" in the minds of some began to gain prominence, due in no small part to the growth of sports outlets on TV, including ESPN, ESPN2, Fox Sports, Outdoor Life Network, etc. Just as was the case with news, sports programming now needed more fodder for its insatiable 24/7 broadcast schedule demands. We started to see "extreme" sports become more prominent and its participants move from the ranks of amateurs to those of professional.

Extreme sports can loosely be defined as athletic activities that involve a combination of high speeds, stunts and, for lack of a better term, massive outputs of adrenaline. Examples of extreme sports include a variety of activities from surfing to in-line skating to BMX (bicycle motocross). The traditional "three sport rotation" of baseball in the summer, football in the fall and basketball in winter no longer dominates the airwaves to the exclusion of other, less traditional "sports." And in many of these sports, enthusiasts began to think of themselves as participants more than just fans.

In addition, some sports that have traditionally seemed to exist at the cultural or regional margins of American life have begun to appeal to a

Pit crew in action during a typical NASCAR race where sponsor logos are predominant.

wider audience. A good example is rodeo. As the following statistics make clear, rodeo reaches a relatively affluent audience with traditional values.

Rodeo Demographics

—78% have household income of $50,000+ annually.

—70% own their own home.

—63% attended college.

—65% are white, 24% are Hispanic, 8% are black.

—74% are ages 18-49.

- For 21 years rodeo has been "the event" attended by truck owners:

  —69% own a domestic truck.

  —51% own more than four vehicles within a single household.

- Rodeo is tradition, patriotism, and family entertainment.

- Actual sales on-site are a mainstay of the program.

- Due to its grass-roots marketing nature, rodeo serves as perfect platform for training and launching of new vehicles.

- Rodeo attendance and viewership has tripled since 1995.

- Rodeo, while typically an agriculturally focused sport, has events all across the country.

- Rodeo is already immersed in Diversity initiatives.

Action shot of Dodge-sponsored rodeo. Dodge sponsors more than 600 rodeos across the country each year, testifying to the growth in the sport's popularity.

Audience segmentation

In pre-World War II America, marketers could pretty much depend on a relatively homogeneous audience. That was never really the case, of course. Although the ratios have changed, the United States has always had racial and cultural diversity. We just never properly acknowledged it, because our visual media reflected what advertisers perceived to be their uniform audience—white males (and, to some extent, females).

All that has changed. Today, the fastest-growing demographic group in the United States is not northern Europeans, but Hispanics, with other ethnic groups not far behind. Racial and ethnic minorities represent blocs of purchasing power that no retailer can ignore and hope to stay in business.

Today, no marketing executive in his or her right mind would overlook the need to appeal to a highly segmented and culturally diverse audience through a variety of approaches. Event marketing provides the flexibility to do this under the umbrella of a single event, unlike traditional advertising media. I'll examine the multicultural phenomenon and its consequences for event marketers further in a later section of this book. For now, suffice it to say that the multicultural audience commands the attention of any serious marketing program.

Mobility

The 1939 New York World's Fair took place, oddly enough, in New York. It wasn't a highly transportable exhibition. If you wanted to see the World's Fair, you had to travel to New York, a doubtful prospect for probably 90 percent of a population that was still highly rural, and, while not impoverished, probably had little discretionary income for such a trip. Special events started to become practical only when large numbers of people were able to come to them.

The expansion of the travel industry—especially after the intro-

"It's better to own an event than to rent one."

Cosponsorships are important to the success of an event. They provide variety and interest for your attendees and help to offset event costs. For the sponsoring company, being part of the event pro-  vides visibility to "captive" target markets, an opportunity to showcase products within a friendly context of other non-competitive sponsors, and the ability to save money by not having to underwrite the total cost of an event.

Nevertheless, when your company's name is on the event, that's the name customers will remember. And it's all about memorability.

duction of jet air travel—made it easier for middle-class America to go farther, faster and cheaper than previous generations had ever dreamed. With the real and psychological barriers to travel dismantled, event marketing became more feasible. Today, thousands of Jeep owners think nothing of traveling across the country to participate in Camp Jeep, something that *would* have been unthinkable not too many years ago. To take this point to another level, PT Cruiser owners demand the ability to be mobile and make more road trips a rite of passage for their events such as the PT Block Party sponsored by the Chrysler brand for their PT Cruiser owners. PT Cruiser clubs have popped up around the country so that fellow Cruisers can gather, meet and hit the road to their favorite music tunes, while enjoying the freedom to express their passion for the driving life.

Affluence

Although it may not seem like it to many of us who would rather be on the golf course but seem to be putting in longer hours on the job, we have more leisure time now than we used to. We also have more money, more disposable income. Not only does this allow us to be a society of consumers, it also allows us the freedom to indulge our lifestyle preferences. This combination of circumstances creates fertile ground for the event marketer, who can appeal to our lifestyle options with product-oriented happenings that he or she can have confidence we will participate in, because we have the time and money to do it.

And that goes for our kids, too. In fact, an entire generation is coming into economic power raised on interactive participation as a large part of its collective experience. Think of TV shows like MTV's *Real World* and its Spring Break specials, not to mention the rash of reality-based TV shows in the *Survivor* and *Fear Factor* genre. In these shows, the line between performer and participant blurs to the point of interchangeability.

Aerial photo of PT Block Party held in Pamona, California, November 2003.

Consumerism

Henry Ford famously said that customers could have any color Model-T that they wanted, so long as it was black. As hard as it is to believe today, that attitude prevailed, not only in the auto industry, but in most other commercial enterprises as well, right into the 1960s. Companies created products—often with little or no input from the consumers who would eventually use them—and made them available for sale. Take it or leave it, the product developers seemed to be saying, knowing that consumers would take it because they had little choice.

Then, for a number of reasons, the tide shifted. Part of it had to do with foreign competition; part of it was due to consumer activism. Whatever it was, the customer was beginning to have options. Manufacturers could no longer ignore the wants and needs of consumers as they developed their new products. Consumers were now having a say in how safely things were built and, since more choices were available, they also were having a say in terms of style. Truth-in-advertising laws and other consumer-friendly regulations were enacted. In other words, even if at the beginning it was only on a very small scale, consumers were *participating* in how products were made and marketed.

That emphasis on consumer participation was also something that event marketers could leverage much more easily than other forms of advertising. As marketing expert Mark Curran points out in *Special Events* magazine, "Advertising, for example, is kind of a one-way message. The Internet has changed a lot of things, not the least of which is [that] consumers have a lot more power, in the sense of having access to information, that they didn't have before. So there is much more of a consumer landscape of choice than existed previously. Therefore, I think it is really important to appeal to audiences in as personal and individual a way as possible. And so I do believe events create a forum or platform [where] there can be a meaningful brand interaction that most brands are trying to have."

Technology

Simply put, technology has transformed the event environment from one of static appreciation by the audience to one of dynamic participation. Multimedia capability, interactivity, super graphics, superb production values—all of these and more have combined to dramatically improve the event attendee's experience. The evolution from observer to participant has been pivotal. It makes the consumer's exposure to the product immediate and memorable, creating a bond that other forms of advertising could not hope to achieve. Computer technology has also improved the event marketer's ability to capture consumer input and measure an event's effectiveness.

Just the improvement in logistics afforded by technology has been significant. It facilitates things like on-line registration, data capture, exhibit design and vendor communications.

The search for authenticity

If a predominant social trend exists among today's consumers, it is the desire for authenticity in all phases of their existence. We see it in everything from television programming to summer camps to our preference in elected officials. People want experiences that peel away artificiality and pretense. They want the real thing, or as near to the real thing as they can get. Event marketing satisfies this demand more completely than any other form of marketing. By bringing consumers into direct contact with products—providing a product immersion—marketers give prospective buyers an undiluted and unmediated experience that is more real and, therefore, more trustworthy.

In the past, special events were often thought of as no more than fluff, a lot of glitz and flash, but with no real substance. They were often seen as a way of distracting the consumer from the less-than-worthy product offerings the special event was meant to support. Among some marketers, this led to skepticism about the value of event marketing, and with good reason. Why persist in doing something that consumers found insincere at best and perhaps even deceptive?

As we will see, consumers have done a complete one-eighty in terms of their perceptions of event marketing. They now see it as an opportunity for the authentic experience. Just ask any of the participants in "Camp Jeep."

Message fatigue

Finally, much of the growing influence of "experience based, access driven marketing," as B. Joseph Pine II and James H. Gilmore refer to it in their book, *The Experience Economy: Work is Theatre & Every Business Is a Stage*, derives from the fact that consumers have been inundated by traditional advertising nearly to the point of apathy. In a monograph called "Promotion Marketing," Zipatoni's Jim Holbrook notes that the proliferation of new products has spawned an "exponential increase in the number of traditional media outlets. There are now more than 1,300 broadcast TV stations; in 1955 there were 441. There are another 1,300-plus cable TV stations; in 1970 there were six. The number of radio stations rose more than 1,000 between 1980 and 2000 to 8,929. There are nearly 10,000 magazines in circulation. And that just covers traditional media." Talk about clutter!

Holbrook goes on to point out that the 72.4 million websites on the Internet provide the platform for millions of additional advertising messages. Citing *Advertising Age*, Holbrook notes that, in all, the average consumer is exposed to nearly 5,000 advertising messages every day. Is it any wonder that many of us tune most of those messages out? In contrast to this sensory bombardment, the experiential event offers consumers an emotional connection to the product that actually helps them make a decision about purchasing it.

The Credibility Factor

Closely related to the previous two trends is the issue of how credible the unending stream of daily commercial messages is. As Al and Laura authors point out in their book *The Fall of Advertising & the Rise of PR*, one of traditional advertising's major drawbacks is consumer skepticism regarding advertising messages. Even if consumers respond to the ads as art, the Rieses note, that doesn't necessarily equate to sales. In fact, often, the more positive the response is to the ad as art, the more negative is the ad's effectiveness in generating sales. The Ries make the case that public relations is a much more credible conveyor of messages because the messengers are presumably objective, third-party, *unpaid* media. They have a convincing argument. Yet, when it comes to credibility, for most people, nothing is more believable than their own senses, their own experiences of products. Once again, that intimate experience with the product is the huge advantage of event marketing.

Whereas traditional advertising through the various mass media has diluted itself by virtue of its own proliferation, event marketing succeeds through the intimate relationship between the customer and the product.

Okay, enough background. In the next chapter we'll look at how to determine when event marketing is the appropriate vehicle for reaching consumers, and how ideas for events begin to take shape.

Chapter Checklist

Checklist

- While special events such as ceremonies and displays have existed for centuries, several cultural trends have contributed to the growth of "experiential" event marketing. These include:

  - The growth of the entertainment industry
  - The evolution of professional sports
  - Audience segmentation
  - Mobility
  - Affluence
  - Consumerism
  - Technology
  - The search for authenticity
  - Message fatigue
  - The credibility factor

Chapter 3
The Strategic Event Game Plan

"We are what we think. All that we are arises with our thoughts. With our thoughts we make the world."

— Siddhartha Gautama (Buddha),
The Dhammapada

Football coaches will tell you that no matter how skilled your players are, without the proper preparation—a game plan—your team is at the mercy of circumstances. Execution on the field is critical, but it is the planning—the practices, skull sessions, the coaches' meetings and the seemingly endless viewing of game films—that determines the execution. Sports analogies are often trite and sometimes even meaningless, but in this case the analogy works. In event marketing, as in most athletic contests, you need a game plan.

Event marketing has proven to be an effective tool for bringing consumers into a direct, experiential relationship with products. The emotional bond that forms when a driver experiences the adrenaline rush of an off-road course in a Jeep, for example, creates a powerful incentive to purchase. Nevertheless, event marketing is not always the most practical, cost-effective or motivating approach to take when trying to market products to consumers.

In addition, in most businesses, the other marketing approaches—advertising, public relations, direct sales—are competing with event marketing for their shares of scarce marketing dollars.

59

So, how do you know when to recommend an event? It becomes a judgment call at some point, but a few guidelines will help in the decision-making process.

Situation analysis

Before embarking on any marketing approach, a number of factors must be considered. This process of consideration is called the *situation analysis*, a thorough and systematic "cost-benefit" assessment of your objectives and the best strategies and tactics to meet those objectives. It will identify benefits and challenges of the proposed event. A situation analysis will look at factors such as the following:

• **Budget**—Event marketing isn't inherently more expensive than any other component of the marketing mix. Just think of the cost of a 60-second TV spot during the Super Bowl. However, as the size and complexity of an event increases, the costs can increase exponentially. The bigger the event, the more logistical considerations must be addressed. This involves vendors and suppliers providing everything from transportation to catering, to equipment rentals to security. Larger events require a bigger footprint or more floor space and have more complex communications needs. Entertainment—everything from concert performances by top-drawer acts to media hospitality receptions—adds to the price of an event, as does travel and lodging. Then there are the costs of advertising and publicizing the event, which can include fees to agencies that specialize in these disciplines. A smaller event on a company's site will reduce some of these costs, and it's possible to handle advertising and public relations internally. Still, cost is a significant factor, requiring that your objective be worth the expenditure.

• **Overall marketing strategy**—In determining whether the objective is worth the expenditure, it is important to ensure that event marketing aligns with and supports a business's overall marketing strategy. Is there a direct cause-and-effect relationship between the proposed event and the achievement of part or all of your marketing strategy? If the event you are proposing appears to be more "fluff" than an integral part of your strategy, you probably need to rethink it.

• **Corporate messages and image**—Will the event support corporate messages and help enhance the corporate reputation? Are there any incongruities between how your various audiences perceive the event and how the company has determined it wants to be perceived? If so, they need to be addressed and reconciled.

• **Current market position**—Is the timing right for event marketing? If you've met 99 percent of your marketing objectives for the year, it might be better to put off any large events until next year, when the need for the impact an event can deliver might be more critical. Can your sales goals be accomplished more quickly and economically through traditional advertising? Does your product lend itself to interaction with large numbers of people? If the product can't support an event on its own, maybe cosponsorship opportunities are worth looking into.

• **Current economic conditions**—Are consumers in a buying mood? We can identify trends in consumer spending and track levels of consumer confidence and other economic indicators. Again, timing is a factor. In some economic environments, marketing events might return their investments, whereas they might not be cost-effective in others. Events don't take place in a vacuum. You might have created the most sensational event in the history of the discipline, but in a poor economy, pocketbook issues may dictate consumer behavior.

- **Consumers**—To whom are you trying to appeal with your event? Do they represent the types of people who are likely to attend the kind of event you are planning? Are they willing to travel out of their way? Are they willing to expend the time necessary to experience your event? What are your customers' lifestyle preferences, the passion points that you can appeal to with your product's attributes? Have you qualified your customers to the extent that you can be reasonably assured they are in the market for your product?

- **Product availability**—Nothing is more frustrating for motivated buyers than to have products unavailable for delivery. Do you anticipate any disruptions of the supply chain, any problems with low inventory? If so, perhaps you need to rethink the timing of the event, especially if your event involves the introduction of new products.

- **Marketing capacity**—Does your company or organization have not only the budget, but also the expertise and the "arms and legs" to pursue event marketing? As I've suggested, event marketing has advanced in sophistication to the point that those managing them should have professional experience in the discipline. Managers need to know how to negotiate with vendors, understand contracts, have a sense of scale and generally know what works and what doesn't. Events also require staffing—people to set up and break down displays and exhibits, to serve as hosts and guides, to register attendees and to perform a variety of other tasks. If you don't have the staff for these activities, you may need to hire temporary staff or use event management agencies.

- **Selling senior management**—Even if the situation analysis seems to favor holding the event, it will still often be necessary to convince senior management of the event's value. Because special events have historically been perceived as "soft" marketing activities—to the extent that they have been recognized as marketing activities at all—a strong prejudice still exists that they don't return the investment of time and money that they require. It will be important to be able to define how you will measure the success of an event so that the expectations of senior management will be realistic. In this respect, the old adage of "underpromise, overdeliver" is the most prudent approach.

Where do the ideas come from?

Okay, you've conducted a thorough situation analysis and you've convinced the CEO (and CFO) that a marketing event will be an effective way to get your customers "up close and personal" with your products. Now all you have to do is come up with an idea for the event. You thought that would be the easy part, but now you find yourself scratching your head and saying to yourself, "What are we going to do?"

After all, you've got a lot of competition out there. Thousands of marketing events take place each year. The event landscape has become every bit as cluttered as the more traditional advertising arenas. But you're actually competing not only with other businesses trying to attract consumers to their events, but also with other entertainment activities. Just check the newspaper events calendar of any major metropolitan area on any given weekend. You'll find a mind-boggling agenda of sporting events, concerts, plays, movies, gallery openings, sales, fairs, flea markets, festivals and other enticements. And this doesn't take into account the normal responsibilities that people have to meet in their day-to-day lives. Their time is extremely limited and they've got a lot of activities competing for their attention. In other words, they have lives. So, what are you going to do to make them want to disrupt those lives to attend your event?

First, we have to go back to those changes in cultural values we talked about above. Any event you plan must satisfy the needs and aspirations of consumers. That takes priority even over the need for the event to align with and support your marketing strategy. As I've discussed, those consumer needs and aspirations include participation and interactivity. You need to appeal to the senses in a way that stands out from the competition. And you need to create an event environment that is receptive to your customers' values. In today's segmented, diversified marketplace, that means you can't be everything to everybody.

Here's another way to think about it. At one polar extreme you have the concept of the carnival. At a garden-variety carnival, the activities are designed to appeal to a wide spectrum of tastes. Opportunities for entertainment include rides, arcades, demonstrations (fortune tellers, magicians, mime troupes and jugglers, perhaps), food and drink, shows, exhibits and other attractions. What you won't typically find at a carnival is any unifying theme. It's just a bunch of unconnected thrills with no objective beyond encouraging attendance and spending. Unfortunately, there was a time when most marketing events resembled carnivals.

Today, however, marketing events are at the other end of the spectrum. They do have an objective, usually to encourage participants to purchase a specific product, often a product not even available at the event. We can think of modern event marketing more in terms of theater productions than carnivals. Indeed, the subtitle of Pine and Gilmore's *The Experience Economy is Work Is Theatre & Every Business a Stage*. Like a play, the marketing event has a central theme, a series of related activities comparable to acts and scenes, a recognizable setting (a carnival, of course, can be plopped down anywhere), often a narrative flow, and even the equivalent of actors assigned to certain roles. And it's all coordinated, which, again, differentiates it from the casual, disjointed structure of the carnival. People often speak of the *architecture* of a dramatic piece, and this sense of architecture or design reflects back on our image of the marketing event as a cosmic spiderweb. I don't believe we'd think of a carnival in terms as elegant as that.

The point is, you don't host an event just to entertain. You host it to engage a target audience emotionally, just as a theatrical production would. The one drawback of the theater analogy, of course, is that, traditionally, the audience doesn't interact in any obvious way with the production. It just observes. But as we've already discussed, even that is changing. If you don't think so, try taking in a performance of Blue Man Group to find out what "audience participation" is all about.

Event themes

A word or two more about themes as they apply to event marketing. Themes not only function as unifying structures for your event. They should also relate strongly to the passion points of your target audience. Take, for example, the annual Sturgis Motorcycle Rally. This is an event that has grown almost organically over the years. It wasn't created by a bunch of suits sitting in a conference room. And it doesn't appear to have an "official" theme. However, it wouldn't be too hard to come up with one. The rally celebrates a very specific lifestyle, a lifestyle that worships the open road and the freedom and independence of the motorcycle. That there's also a hint of the outlaw in the theme—based on the public perception of large groups traveling on motorcycles going all the way back to Marlon Brando in *The Wild Ones*—also doesn't hurt. These "passion points" are reflected in the event's activities, which include everything from country-rock bands (whose anthems are traditionally "outlaw" in motif) to motorcycle races.

Pine and Gilmore point out that "Theming an experience means scripting a participative story," and they offer five principles that are paramount in developing a "compelling and captivating" theme.

1. "An engaging theme must alter a guest's sense of reality." This of course doesn't mean that the event should induce psychosis. It *does* mean that the event should lift the participant out of his or her everyday experience—it should "enhance the guest's comfort zone."

2. "The richest venues possess themes that fully alter one's sense of reality by affecting the experience of space, time, and matter." In other words, it's not just a change in everyday activities. The venue should reflect the theme by modifying the dimensions of the environment. We'll look at this more closely in the chapter on "Eye Candy."

3. "Engaging themes integrate space, time, and matter into a cohesive, realistic whole." Not only are the dimensions of space, time and matter manipulated, but they are subordinated to the unity of the theme. The Hard Rock Cafés offer a good example of this integration. Everything contributes to the rock-and-roll theme, from the naming of the entrées to the décor and memorabilia.

4. "Themes are strengthened by creating multiple places within a place." An event such as DaimlerChrysler's Route 2003 illustrates this rule perfectly. Within the overall Route 2003 venue are sub-venues such as off-road courses, race courses, full-size exhibits and games.

5. "A theme should fit the character of the enterprise staging the experience." Consistency is important. A massage booth at a golf show seems appropriate. It seems less appropriate—therefore inconsistent—at an auto show. This rule, it seems, gets broken more than most. Someone always thinks that an exhibition of belly dancers might be a nice thing to have, no matter that it might have nothing even close to do with the theme of the event itself.

If you've gotten to this point in your development of an idea for an event, you are thinking of an activity that is unified thematically, that appeals to your specific audience on an experiential level, and that is integrated with your overall marketing strategy. Now, when we come back to the original question—"Where do the ideas come from?"—your options have been limited somewhat. But that's good. You can now see your way more clearly to the kind of event you need to be thinking about. You have a starting point, the beginning of a blueprint. The problem is, where do you go from here?

Establish the event brief

The event brief, informed by the marketing objectives and strategies, provides the raw material for developing the creative ideas for the event. A typical event brief will identify target audiences, outline the proposed program, project the strategic vision for the targeted segment, and define the brand and its appropriateness to the targeted segment. It will also locate the product passion points, explain what the program offers, and look at the potential challenges.

The event brief also should detail objectives. Our event brief for the Camp Jeep event, for example, estimates the number of attendees and test drives based on a careful analysis of previous Camp Jeep experience. Relevant budget issues should also be covered in the event brief, along with an explanation of measurement methodology. Finally, other event requirements should be included, such as creative needed and potential cosponsorships.

Okay, but again, where do the ideas come from?

Despite the many different theories about creativity, nobody has yet explained definitively where it comes from. Traditionally, people have accepted the "You're either born with it, or you're not" assumption. Creative people are perceived as "dreamy," "imaginative," perhaps even "gifted." Unfortunately, words that typically are *not* uttered in the same breath as creative are "practical," "logical" or "realistic" (this last term is used especially when referring to budgetary limits). Creative is "right brain"; the opposite of creative is "left brain." In the minds of most people, this "either/or" situation prevails to the extent that many of us, assuming we aren't creative by birthright, just shrug our shoulders and assume we'll need to get into "left brain" careers like engineering and accounting. However, in the field of event marketing, creativity must be grounded in reality if it is to be successful. And reality in this case means tying your creative idea back to the brand or product strategy and your marketing objectives. Once again, the concept of the cosmic spiderweb comes to mind: artistry married to utility.

I often think that creativity isn't so much a matter of some magical endowment as it is a matter of attitude. One of my first tasks when I was hired by Chrysler was to domesticate the then-novel concept of the minivan to consumers, especially women. Many women had the same initial reaction to the idea of driving around a minivan that my wife had at the time: "No way am I going to drive a van," she said with conviction. Her reluctance wasn't hard to understand. At that time, vans were 12-passenger trucks and the van conversion rage was just beginning. The intensity of this reaction sent me in search of how other women looked at the prospect of driving a van. I learned that they had "issues" with vans, issues they verbalized as, for example, having to step too high to get into the driver's seat or needing more extension of the hood to provide better depth perception.

At the time, my children were young enough—and I was old enough—to appreciate the wisdom and humor of *The Muppet Show* which we occasionally watched on TV together. One day, it hit me. Using the the Muppets characters as a way of literally bringing home the benefits of the minivan would be a great way to introduce the minivan to an audience still skittish about the "van's" connotation and image as a handyman's conveyance.

My team and I came up with the idea of creating a Muppets movie set that we would take on a 40-city, mall tour, the mall environment being ideally suited for the targeted audience. The set would occupy the middle of these malls and would contain miniature Voyager vans on tracks that kids could sit in and ride. Along the route of this ride, they would learn about traffic safety rules from robotically animated Muppet characters, with safety for their children the operative issue for parents. That's right. Robotically animated Muppet characters. Well, you can imagine Jim Henson's reaction when I first presented the idea to him. He was not receptive, to put it mildly. Jim was a true puppeteer, that is to say, a true artist, and I'm sure the thought of using his creations to demonstrate the positive features of Chrysler's minivans smacked too much of commercialism. Over months of many meetings and intense discussions, the benefit of the program's mission to teach children safety messages that could carry over for years became clear. Once he "experienced" the children and parents interacting, Henson came to love the exhibit.

We were satisfying a couple of needs. We brought the event to a location that was included within our audience's daily routines, we brought education to their children about a fact of life in their growing up, we addressed an issue that was a major factor in automotive accidents (children being hurt), and we delivered the message in an entertaining and relevant communication through the use of the Muppets, with their reputation for quality, truth and believability. But for the program to really work, both the Chrysler/Plymouth brand and the Muppet brand managers needed a common bond: Keep kids safe and informed. The result was an award-winning exhibit that traveled for three years around the country earning plaudits from parents, organizations and government agencies.

I relate this story not to tout my own creative abilities but to make a point about attitude as it relates to creativity in developing events. That attitude has to do with confidence, persistence and, maybe more important than anything else, the willingness to be alert to what's around you—to trust in and use your experience—in developing ideas. Often, things that seem to have no apparent relationship—the Muppets and minivans, for example—can combine to spark a blockbuster idea.

Lou Bitonti

Look at precedents

One way of getting the creative juices flowing is to do some research. What has your company done in the past by way of marketing events? In what ways have they succeeded or failed? What about the successes and failures of other companies, both peer companies and those with entirely different businesses? We all want to be original, of course, but it's important not to overlook the way other organizations have done things. If it's true that there are really no new ideas in the universe, then it may be very helpful to look to the good ideas that others have come up with as departure points. There may be ways of modifying or adapting those great ideas that will work very well for your product. You must become a student of people; look at the way people act or react; expand your curiosity, because it fuels creativity. In other words, become a people-watcher with a purpose.

Lou Bitonti (left) Kermit the Frog, Jim Henson and Jim Jandasek at the press conference for the introduction of the highly acclaimed Jim Henson's Muppet Safety Tour, sponsored by the Plymouth brand, Chrysler Corporation.

Brainstorming

This time-honored creative process deserves its place in the pantheon of idea generators. Getting three or four people in a room and letting them have complete freedom to throw out ideas is an excellent way to break through complacency and creative blocks. In a brainstorming session, one idea feeds off or builds upon another, often with very exciting results. And, because it's an inclusive process, everyone gets a sense of ownership of the final idea, which promotes the critical sense of teamwork necessary to successful events.

Brainstorming guidelines

The guidelines for brainstorming vary, but the following are typical:

• *Identify a leader or facilitator.* It helps to have someone in control so that the stronger personalities in the room don't monopolize or criticize, which discourages the entire brainstorming process. The facilitator also keeps the session running on time and may serve as the person who records ideas, preferably using a blackboard, whiteboard or flipchart so that everybody can see them.

• *Speaking of time, set a time limit.* Establishing a time limit—60 minutes is a reasonable chunk of time for busy people—helps participants to focus on the task.

• *Define the issue or problem.* Everyone should agree on the definition before the session starts. Write it out where everybody can see it.

• *Encourage participants to offer their ideas aloud.* Everyone should feel uninhibited enough to spout off the craziest notions that enter their heads. Discourage self-censorship.

• *No one is allowed to criticize, comment on or react in any way to ideas as they are being generated and recorded.* This is the very essence of brainstorming and is, therefore, of extreme importance.

• *Participants should feel free to build on previously stated ideas.* This is another key benefit of brainstorming—creative cross-fertilization.

• *Some experts on brainstorming recommend that, when the session is over, the original brainstorming group participants select the top three (or five or 10) ideas, vote on them and prioritize according to the vote.* Other experts contend that the brainstorming session is over once all the ideas have been generated, that selecting ideas from the pool is another process. In either case, it's important to recognize that part of the process is creative and another part is analytical, and they require two different mental approaches.

Finally, if you don't have a large group, brainstorming works well as an individual technique, too. Indeed, several brainstorming software programs are available that allow people to brainstorm individually using their computers.

Consult the experts

If you have advertising and public relations experts on staff, or access to them through agency relationships, this is a good time to call on their expertise. It is the rare public relations professional or advertising executive who has not had some experience with event marketing in his or her career. Grand openings, corporate anniversaries, product launches, conferences, seminars and other events are part of the repertoire of the advertising and public relations world, so if you are able to draw on this experience base, you shouldn't hesitate to do so.

Review the literature

To truly understand event marketing, one needs to read, read, and then read some more. Articles, trends, research—anything can lead to formulating an idea or supporting an events plan. Having access to PR avenues can help ideas reach the table.

People and organizations that host successful marketing events usually like to let other people know about it. They write about them in their trade publications and submit them to competitions for the coveted prizes in their respective professional societies. For example, the Public Relations Society of America (PRSA), the world's largest organization for public relations practitioners, lists on its Website (www.prsa.org) more than 200 past winners of its Silver Anvil prize in the special events category—everything from Celebrating 40 Years of Barbie Doll Dreams to The Rock and Roll Hall of Fame & Museum Groundbreaking. At this site, each of the events is described in detail along with methodologies and rationales.

Additional organizations that use awards to recognize excellence in event marketing include:

- The PMA Reggie Awards (http://www.pmalink.org/awards/reggie/competition/default.asp)

- *The Event Marketer Magazine* Ex Awards (http://www.eventmarketermag.com/exawards/index.html)

- The *Promo Magazine* ProAwards (http://www.promomagazine.com)

Sites like these are gold mines of ideas that can be adapted to your own marketing event.

Benchmarking

A more systematic approach to the "review of the literature" described above is *benchmarking*. As with the use of the term *brainstorming*, *benchmarking* gets thrown around a lot by people who don't necessarily understand the function. It is more than just "seeing how we stack up against our competitors." In *The Benchmarking Book*, author Michael J. Spendolini defines benchmarking as follows: "A continuous, systematic process for evaluating the products, services and work processes of organizations that are recognized as representing best practices for the purposes of organizational improvement." Spendolini points out that his definition seeks to dispel a number of myths about the process.

Benchmarking myths

Benchmarking is a one-time event. Business is, or should be, a fluid, dynamic, ever-changing enterprise. To assume that one exercise in benchmarking will suffice to upgrade your events is not realistic. You need to continuously be scanning the event marketing horizon for new ideas.

Benchmarking provides solutions. Benchmarking does not mean that you simply graft onto your event the best practices of some other event. Benchmarking *does* mean that you adopt, modify and integrate best practices as they best meet the needs of your event.

Benchmarking is copying or imitating. Whereas the critics of benchmarking see it as simple mimicry of one organization by another, Spendolini points out that more useful terms to apply are *assimilate* and *pragmatic* as in "learning from others and applying that knowledge to one's own business practices in a practical manner."

Benchmarking is quick and easy. While it isn't a necessarily difficult process, benchmarking requires planning, discipline, analysis and time—just like a lot of worthwhile business processes.

Benchmarking is a fad. Benchmarking has been integrated into the organizational activities of some of the top companies in the United States, including Xerox, Motorola and IBM. The process is seen as a significant contributor to quality and as a stimulus to continuous improvement. Corporate America is not likely to abandon something that adds as much value as benchmarking.

There are a number of theories on benchmarking, including theories on how many steps the benchmarking process should have. Spendolini simplifies the process by identifying five benchmarking steps. These are:

1. Determine *what* to benchmark. The benchmarking process is not a "hit or miss" activity. It is important to have a good idea of what you want to benchmark before starting. In other words, what are the objectives of your benchmarking project? Do you want to know how other companies are streamlining logistics? Or, how about what's being done in interactive displays? Maybe you want to know both. If so, you have two benchmarking projects.

2. *Form* a benchmarking team. Just as you put together a core team for events (more about core teams in the next chapter), the benchmarking process should be a team activity. And, just as you assemble your core team by looking for a diversity of talents, expertise and personalities, the same mix is required for the benchmarking team. In fact, probably the best way to approach this process is to form a task force from the core team to do the benchmarking. They will already know the relevance of what is learned for your proposed event, which will help them to focus in on pertinent information.

3. *Identify* benchmark partners. You want to identify best practices, right? Well, a good place to start is to look at those companies that are winning the awards in event marketing. You can also attend as many events as possible to determine what's new and exciting in event marketing. Spendolini also recommends monitoring the media, especially the trade publications to see what other companies are up to, using professional organizations as sources for best practices information, paying attention to word-of-mouth recommendations and hiring consultants who can direct you to the resources and information you need.

4. *Collect and analyze* benchmarking information. Benchmarking data can be obtained through a number of channels, including interviews, site visits, surveys, media analysis and archival research. Analysis basically translates into understanding the relevance and application of a best practice to your own event needs. As was mentioned earlier, this usually means something more dynamic than simply grafting an event component.

5. Take *action*. Benchmarking is a dynamic process. A benchmarking report that sits on a shelf doesn't achieve its objective. On the other hand, you may find that an organization has nothing to offer you at the present. Taking action suggests adapting and incorporating into your event those best practices that meet a real need.

Benchmarking is not so much a process of imitation as it is an effort to improve through what might be called modeling, analogous to the "performance" or "role modeling" espoused by self-help guru Tony Robbins. The nuance is important. It suggests that you use the best of the best practices and make them your own. That, in turn, means transforming an idea and making it better. It's a process that will help to keep your events new and interesting.

Innovate

Maybe you've already arrived at a successful formula for marketing events for your business, something you can use repeatedly because it supports product loyalty. Some events, such as the annual pilgrimage to Sturgis and Camp Jeep have become perennial favorites for thousands of consumers. If your event has achieved this level of success, your challenge now is to keep it fresh. Perhaps a change of venue would enliven the event. If that's not feasible (it wouldn't be for an event like Sturgis, for example) perhaps a change in the entertainment lineup would be in order. Keep in mind that tremendous competition exists for the attention of your customers, and if your event begins to stale even a bit, their attention may drift elsewhere.

Measurement

Finally, it's important to have a reliable measurement tool to evaluate the effectiveness of your event. This is true for all components of the marketing mix, but perhaps even more so for event marketing, which is basically the new kid on the block and has yet to fully prove its accountability in terms of return on investment. As Kurt Miller writes in Jack Morton's *360° Newsletter*, "Clearly, marketers need to do a better job of measuring performance, and in turn, of using the resulting information to truly prove the performance of their future event programs. Ultimately, they have everything to gain—plus a lot to lose."

We'll discuss measurement in greater detail later in this book. For now, just remember that a marketing approach is only as effective as the methods you use to measure it. Measurement isn't the sexiest part of event marketing, so it's often overlooked, underappreciated or even consciously avoided. But effective measurement can make the difference between an event marketing program's continuation or demise.

If you've gotten this far in the process, you've completed your situation analysis and determined that event marketing is the approach you want to take to meet a specific marketing objective. You've convinced senior management of the benefits of the approach through the event brief you have developed, created an idea that works within the budget and established a system of measuring the effectiveness of the event. Now it's time to start "spinning the web."

Case Study: Microsoft's launch of Xbox

One of the most keenly anticipated product launches in recent marketing history was Microsoft's November 2001 launch of its first game console—Xbox. Microsoft claimed that Xbox had more power than any game console then on the market and the company matched that power with the largest marketing budget for a game console in history. It was an ambitious launch, geared to a gamer audience with high expectations, and GMR Marketing, the company chosen to design and implement that launch, created a series of marketing events equal to the magnitude of the occasion.

The launch was actually separated into three phases: pre-launch, which commenced in May 2000, a year-and-a-half before the actual launch date; launch day, November 15, 2001; and, post-launch, the ongoing brand penetration and migration to new markets.

The objectives of the comprehensive program were threefold:

1. To generate, validate and sustain consumer "buzz" about Xbox among all game audiences

2. To drive total market awareness of the Xbox console and games among retailers, game publishers and the media

3. To drive sales and ongoing brand engagement

These three objectives roughly corresponded to the three phases of the launch strategy. In developing the actual launch plan, GMR researched and brokered entertainment and venue partnerships, potential promotion partnerships, designed and produced all the technical components and fully integrated the plan with advertising, public relations, retail and direct marketing initiatives.

Prelaunch activities:

• *Seeking to jump-start buzz about Xbox*, Microsoft staged a two-day entertainment and promotional event at the Experience Music Project in Seattle to tantalize key retailers and media. Activities included a high-impact, multimedia preview of Xbox and featured a performance by comic magicians Penn & Teller, along with musical entertainment.

• *With the 2001 Electronic Entertainment Expo (E3) as a backdrop,* Microsoft further stimulated interest in Xbox by designing and managing a 20,000-square-foot Xbox gaming pod and coordinating featured performances by Blink 182 and Third Eye Blind.

• *Prelaunch activities culminated in a promotion* to stimulate consumer trial and encourage purchase, featuring a 48-hour, nonstop gaming marathon held simultaneously in New York and Los Angeles. With more than 50 gaming kiosks at each venue, consumers could play competitively to win significant prizes. The event featured live performances by Bush and Sevendust. Free food and beverages were provided by co-marketing partners Taco Bell and SoBe. And, to extend the event beyond the confines of these venues, two weeks of radio prepromotions and live, on-site remote broadcasts/on-air contests were scheduled, which provided national coverage reaching four million people.

The launch: midnight madness

Actual launch day consisted of two main events:

"Beware of your comfort zone."

 Like it or not—and most of us seem to like it fine—we are creatures of habit. This can be a good thing. Habitual behavior greatly streamlines our lives by incorporating efficiencies into our day-to-day activities. Just think how chaotic life would be if we had to relearn each of our skills every day.

But in the event marketing world, "comfort" can too easily slip into complacency. To truly be event people, we cannot have anything that is sacred. We must question, measure, attain and upgrade. In other words, we should be in a constant mode of improvement.

- *The first, the product launch itself, occurred one minute after midnight* at the new flagship Toys 'R' Us store in Times Square. In preparation for the event, GMR "lit the Town Green," reflective of the distinctive high-visibility green of the Xbox itself. Green projection lighting was used to illuminate Times Square billboards, and green-glow necklaces were distributed to pedestrians. Hot dog vendors served customers wearing green T-shirts. As part of the actual launch, GMR coordinated with the World Wrestlilng Federation (WWF) to provide a seamless transition from a private release party to the actual retail release (highlighted by Bill Gates facing off against "The Rock" in a game of Temco's popular Dead or Alive 3).

- *To celebrate the launch*, a consumer event was held at the Metronome, one of New York City's premier hot spots. Within this hip environment, which included 40 game stations for guests to try Xbox, more than 4,750 participants engaged in a 48-hour competition, which included:

    —Complimentary Taco Bell and SoBe to keep gamers fueled

    —A Ford Sport Trac truck giveaway with built-in Xbox and LCD screen

    —Appearances by Sevendust and Bush

    —DJs spinning all night long

Postlaunch Xbox Odyssey

To create and maintain consumer and retailer excitement from product launch and beyond, a mammoth mobile marketing attraction and national tour called Xbox Odyssey was unveiled following the launch. The Odyssey featured:

- Two 53-foot semi's that converted into a humongous inflated dome.

- Inside, the domes were fitted out with 52 game stations, a DJ stand and overhead video screens. Cool tunes, game play and a VIP Lounge awaited gamers.

- Gamers had a total of 96 gaming opportunities to compete head-to-head in multiplayer games such as Halo, NFL Fever, DOA3 and Fuzion Frenzy, and one-on-one games such as Tony Hawk 2X, NHL Hitz and Transworld Surf.

This mobile marketing tour reflected the unique Xbox experience; it was flexible to meet multiple needs, environments and audiences and provided the ability to incorporate co-marketing partners and featured titles/developers. Xbox Odyssey rolled to 35 cities across the country, incorporating local flavor at each stop, including:

- Performances by hot local bands

- Local radio station promotions for giveaways, including Xbox consoles and games, VIP party invitations and Xbox promotional materials

- Local artist designs for posters (for distribution to major retailers), stickers (provided to alternative music and action sports shops), T-shirts and lanyards (given to all attendees)

Microsoft continued to support the launch of Xbox via an eight-market, radio-driven promotion designed to make consumers aware of extensive title offerings. (Research had shown incorrect perceptions about the number of games available for Xbox.) Promoters developed 12 "tricked out" Cadillac Escalades with Xbox graphic packages, Bose surround systems, 27-inch TV and Xbox System and a variety of game titles. Ten of the Escalades went to 10 radio stations for in-kind promos. The Escalades were taken to radio station events and guerrilla stops by GMR marketing managers. Each radio station also got Xbox systems and gear to give away, and most gave their Escalades away at the end of the five-week blitz, while one Escalade was also given away through an on-line national sweepstake at www.xbox.com.

Microsoft maintained the trade push with an Xbox "Splash" at the 2002 E3 show. Part of this effort included the design and construction of an amazing 25,000-square-foot, two-story trade show environment with 20 meeting rooms and hundreds of screens. Press and retail VIP briefings were held at the historic Orpheum two days prior to the event, and a hospitality bash was staged the night before the event at the Park Plaza Hotel, with performances by Garbage and others. Finally, Microsoft expanded Xbox's already considerable presence by placing the Xbox Odyssey mobile attraction in downtown Los Angeles for additional meetings and a briefing for financial press.

Results

- Microsoft sold 1.5 million Xbox units in North America between the November 15 launch and the end of calendar year 2001, making the Xbox video game system one of the most successful launches in video game history.

- Gamers bought more than three games with every Xbox system, the highest-ever game attach rate for video game console launch.

The Microsoft Xbox launch event series of activities succeeded because it articulated clear objectives, focused on the passion points of the target audience, and because the program was executed with thoroughness and style. (Xbox case study courtesy of Stephen Knill of GMR Marketing, Inc.)

Chapter Checklist

Checklist

- In determining whether to use event marketing, it is important to conduct a thorough situation analysis that looks at factors such as budget, your overall marketing strategy, the target audience, staffing capacity and current economic conditions,

- In developing event ideas and themes, event marketers need to research the literature, use brainstorming and benchmarking effectively, and should always be seeking to innovate.

- Objectives for the event should be clearly defined going in so that the measurement of the event's effectiveness will be valuable.

Chapter 4
Event Planning and Management
"Spinning the Web"

"Individual commitment to a group effort—that is what makes a team work, a company work, a society work, a civilization work."

— Vince Lombardi, legendary pro football coach

The team approach

I love the theme of teamwork. That's why I like coaching high school football. That's why I like football analogies. You can't do an event without taking a team approach. The person who thinks he or she can do it all by himself or herself will fail miserably. You need what I like to call a "core team," a group of specialists in a variety of disciplines who work together as a cohesive unit to plan and implement the event. Finally, you also need a leader, or coach.

Team leader attributes

The coach analogy is a good one for the event marketing team leader. Just like a football coach, the team leader has to be everything from a strategist to a cheerleader. He or she needs to be able to "see the entire field," in other words, to have the big picture. The team leader needs to understand how all the parts function individually and in harmony with the rest of the parts—how, for example, transportation dovetails with security. This ability to understand the big picture is critical because of the scope and complexity of today's marketing events. Just as a football coach needs to understand both the defensive and offensive options simultaneously on the field, the event marketing team leader must juggle all the various components of the event, anticipating, adapting and course-correcting as required.

Another way to look at it is that the team leader is like a symphony conductor. He or she brings together the various parts of the orchestra into a unified, harmonic whole.

But you shouldn't assume that the team leader is nothing but a command-and-control freak. In addition to his or her technical expertise—the knowledge needed to understand everything from site selection to entertainment to measurement—the team leader also needs to be a little "off center." He or she needs the imagination and flexibility characteristic of "right-brain" types, because, as the concept of the cosmic spiderweb suggests, event marketing is as much an organic process as it is static design. Opportunities and challenges emerge spontaneously when you're dealing with human beings in an event environment, and it often takes imagination and creativity to respond to those opportunities and challenges.

Probably the most important attribute of a good team leader is the ability to recognize the talents and strengths of his or her team members and utilize those talents effectively. Again, the coaching analogy is a good one. As a football coach, you might have a player who is six-six and 250 pounds and who you want to make a tight end. But if the player can't catch the ball or doesn't have the "soft hands" to be an effective position player, you'd better make him a tackle or you're in trouble.

Other team leader qualifications

In addition to having the "big picture"—the 30,000-foot perspective—an effective team leader also needs to be detail-oriented. He or she needs to be immersed in the company's brand strategy, up to speed on the latest technology, and have a sense of "the buzz"—what's current and hot in terms of popular culture and the cultural values of the target audience. A good ear for trends is essential; nothing is worse than being tone-deaf when it comes to the tastes of your customers. Placido Domingo is a great talent, but he probably isn't the right guy to perform at Sturgis.

Then there is the issue of ego. Certainly, an event manager needs to have confidence and self-assurance. He or she needs to command the respect of the core team and a wide variety of other players, just as a coach needs to have the total respect and loyalty of his or her team. But the coach can't overshadow the team. The event manager who thought he or she was just going to wake up one morning and go to a golf tournament, for example, and was going to be the person who presents the oversize check on TV, is in for a big surprise. Nine out of 10 times, the event manager doesn't even get recognized. In fact, if you are the manager and you *do* get recognized, you haven't done your job. The event has to be seamless; customers will see through anything that suggests manipulation or pressure. In the movie *The Recruit*, Al Pacino, playing the veteran CIA recruiter, tells his student agents, "Our failures are known, our successes are not." It's not quite that severe in event marketing, but the principle is the same.

Creating the core team

The core team for a marketing event is really the *planning* team, the unit that helps the event marketing manager create the cosmic spiderweb. Putting the core team together is really the first step in developing the event. While not every organization will have the resources to assemble the team as it is outlined ideally here, the areas of expertise discussed below will need to be addressed. So, who's on the team?

• **The program manager**—The core team leader is primarily responsible for the event. He or she conveys the company's vision, mission and marketing strategy. As I've suggested, the core team leader is like a football coach. He or she has the game plan, the offensive and defensive philosophy and the ability to put the right people at the right positions. The *program manager* is like the quarterback of the football team—the field general. He or she executes the plan. But that doesn't mean he or she doesn't need imagination and creativity. Like a quarterback, the program manager needs to be able to read situations on the ground and adjust to them flexibly. In other words, sometimes he or she has to call audibles and be able to utilize the available resources—human and otherwise—effectively. In the world of event marketing, the program management position typically falls to the full-service advertising agency's event marketing component.

• **The design firm**—Obviously, the visual impact of an event plays a key role in its success. Displays and exhibits—what I like to call "eye candy"— need to be consistent with your marketing objectives, so it's important that your design firm get involved early in the development of the event. Because of the lead time to develop displays and exhibits, designers need to know what's required of them, how the event space is configured, and other essential data as early as possible. And the best way for them to be informed is to sit in on the core team meetings.

• **The financial person**—Because of the importance of budgeting, you need to have a financial person sitting at the table. But it also needs to be the *right* financial person. You don't simply want a bean counter who's going to have financial tunnel vision when it comes to the planning process. A good financial person will bring to the process a firm grasp of the financial resources available and how those resources can be allocated, along with an appreciation of the value of event marketing. If your financial team member is constantly shooting down ideas based solely on cost, showing no flexibility, the overall effect on the team could be discouragement. This is not a good environment for ideas to flourish in. On the other hand, the financial person needs to be a "reality check" for the team, bringing fiscal discipline to the process. The person with this combination of qualities is rare. If you find one, learn to appreciate his or her invaluable contribution.

• **Public relations**—The most spectacular marketing event that nobody knows about is an event that might as well never have happened. And there is no more effective way to generate awareness of and interest in a marketing event than through the use of public relations. The most obvious tool in the public relations arsenal for publicizing marketing events is media relations. When print reporters do stories on your events and electronic reporters do broadcasts *from* your event, you not only get additional exposure for the event, you also get credibility. But public relations doesn't just implement media relations. This discipline can also provide such services as media training for your spokespersons, message development and refinement, the development of collateral print materials, crisis management and communications, and a host of other services. For example, the public relations representatives can do "article searches" to validate a potential element of an event. I'm going to cover the valuable role of public relations in more detail further in this book, but for now, suffice it to say that, in identifying the key members of the core team, none is more important than the public relations person.

• **Advertising**—Of course, not all marketing communications to support your event come via the free media. Because it is important to reach targeted audiences, advertising is also an important tool in raising awareness. Advertising experts know how to create effective ads and schedule them in the appropriate publications at the right time. They have expertise in direct mail and customer relationship management. In fact, the one-two punch of advertising and public relations is a very powerful way to increase awareness of your event. If your company is running a national ad campaign, it's also wise to have the national representative sit in on your core team meetings. He or she can assist with tie-ins and other ways to coordinate advertising messages with your event.

One more note about advertising: One advertising opportunity that hasn't been maximized is the area of commercials about the events themselves. We've seen a few examples of this: Saturn's advertising of its Springhill owner reunion events and MasterCard's emphasis on lifestyle advertising in conjunction with the TV spots for its cards come to mind. But it still lags behind. The ideal event ad would be one that advertises both the event and the product.

• **Legal**—Because of the scale and complexity of marketing events—and the fact that large numbers of people are usually involved—the input of the legal experts is indispensable to the event planning process. As in the case of the financial person, legal counsel can provide a "reality check." They can also provide guidance in terms of company liability and other land mines. Murphy's Law says that if something can go wrong, it will. Event planning should anticipate problems and minimize their occurrence, but even the best planning doesn't guarantee that nothing will go wrong. Legal counsel can supply insight into potential problems with venues, message issues and other key components of the planning process.

• **Research**—Measurement of an event—how effectively it met its objectives, how customers responded to the event's activities and other metrics—is too often an afterthought. As we will see, how well event objectives are defined at the beginning determines how effectively you can measure your event's effectiveness. That's why it's important to have the research team at the core team table. They will know which objectives are realistic, "measurable" and actionable and can provide counsel on how to "sell" an event concept to management. Having the research team involved at the beginning also gives them a head start on developing the research tools and methodologies they will need to perform effectively on-site.

• **Website designers**—Because your website will be one of the primary sources of information on your event, the designers and managers of the site should be involved early in the process. They need to know about event themes and objectives in order to make sure that the Web presence for your event is consistent with off-line sources of information. They'll also need target audience lists and information necessary to conduct on-line registrations, which are becoming more and more important.

• **Logistics**—By definition, logistics takes in a lot of territory. The category includes everything from entertainment selection to site venue to food catering to display transportation. Nothing gets done without effective logistics. It literally represents the implementation of the plan. Logistics experts need to be adept at scheduling, identifying suppliers and vendors, negotiating contracts, working with unions, understanding security issues and a vast range of other activities. To return to our spiderweb analogy once again, the logistics people are the ones who actually make the connections of the filaments, who bring the cosmic spiderweb together.

Under the general category of logistics, you may have additional representatives on the core team, including your travel partner, transportation experts, security consultants and other key vendors.

The trust factor

It's one thing to say that you have gotten together in one room the people with the right qualifications to plan and implement a marketing event. It's quite another to say that you can get them to work together smoothly and harmoniously. Again, this task falls back on the shoulders of the event marketing manager to ensure that he or she not only has people with expertise in the right fields, but the right attitudes as well. This is where things get a bit intangible, but you can't overestimate their importance. The event manager needs to trust that his or her core team will perform, will come through with a solid idea that he or she is willing to implement with confidence and enthusiasm.

The core team's ability to do this is complicated by a number of factors. A core team is made up of different personalities, often personalities that are polar opposites. In fact, sometimes you'll find that you have competing companies in the same room sitting next to each other as members of the core team. Core team members may have different missions and agendas. None of these factors must be allowed to interfere with the process.

What other qualities should the members of your core team have? Well, it would be helpful if they've had some experience in event marketing. They should also have a solid grasp of the organization's marketing objectives and at least a general sense of the marketing strategy. It probably goes without saying that they should have knowledge and understanding of your company's product lines and offerings, but I'll say it anyway.

Finally, your core team needs to be a fearless group. Each member needs to be willing to stand up and be counted in support of the event idea. Members of the core team need to be secure in their abilities, but they also need to be flexible and cooperative. And, basically, that's the definition of a team player.

The strategic event planning process

With the core team in place, you're ready to really dig in to the planning process. A variety of approaches are available, but one very useful guide is a four-step process that helps distill the complexity of mapping an event into obvious stages. Before getting into the four steps, your core group will have already articulated the marketing mission and any planning assumptions that need to be considered.

Step 1: Event categorization

The event marketing purchase funnel on page 96 is a useful tool for this step of the planning process. The funnel charts the purchasing cycle from product *awareness* at the broadest (top) level, and from there, narrowing the purchasing decision process through the *consideration, shopping* and *preference* levels to the ideal point of a sale. The type of event will be dictated by where on the purchase funnel your product finds itself. For a relatively new product, for example, it might be important to cultivate awareness on a broad scale before actually trying to drive sales before the consumer is ready. Conversely, a well-established product might require categorization in a "lower funnel" event where the goal will be to drive qualified traffic and transactions. Ideally, the lower the event is categorized in the purchase funnel, the closer will be the experiential connection between the product and the customer, and the greater will be the likelihood of a sale.

Step 2: Setting objectives/key measures for success

Establishing objectives for the event and quantifying metrics that demonstrate how effectively the event met your objectives is what Step 2 is all about. For example, if your objective is awareness, you could set a goal of a certain number of visitors or attendees and measure that objective by calculating how many people actually show up. Similarly, media exposures qualify as a measurement of awareness. Farther down the purchase funnel, consideration can be measured by consumer surveys or, if you can track it, encounters with the product (such as the number of test drives attendees take). If your surveys and other measures of consideration tell you that attendees are ready to take the next step—shopping—you can start to build qualified traffic, driving them farther down the funnel into the preference area, where more tangible incentives like coupons, sweepstakes and other redemptions can motivate them to sales.

Lou Bitonti

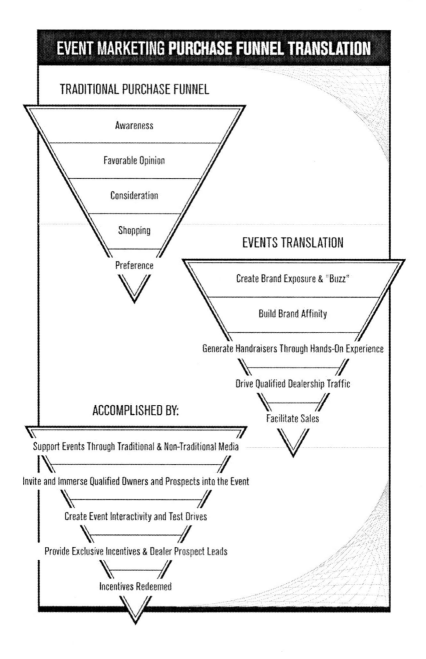

EVENT MARKETING PURCHASE FUNNEL TRANSLATION

TRADITIONAL PURCHASE FUNNEL

- Awareness
- Favorable Opinion
- Consideration
- Shopping
- Preference

EVENTS TRANSLATION

- Create Brand Exposure & "Buzz"
- Build Brand Affinity
- Generate Handraisers Through Hands-On Experience
- Drive Qualified Dealership Traffic
- Facilitate Sales

ACCOMPLISHED BY:

- Support Events Through Traditional & Non-Traditional Media
- Invite and Immerse Qualified Owners and Prospects into the Event
- Create Event Interactivity and Test Drives
- Provide Exclusive Incentives & Dealer Prospect Leads
- Incentives Redeemed

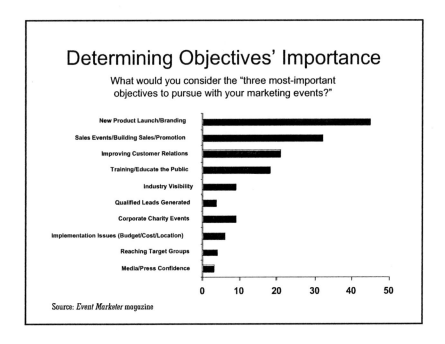

Determining Objectives' Importance

What would you consider the "three most-important objectives to pursue with your marketing events?"

Source: *Event Marketer* magazine

Step 3 — Implementation

Once the event has been categorized and the objectives and metrics are in place, it's time to implement the event. What this entails will depend upon the nature of the event. If it's an event to establish awareness, implementation might include cooperative arrangements with event partners, radio promos and other advertising support. It would also include on-site presence in the form of signage or displays and/or demonstrations. If, on the other hand, you want to build qualified traffic with the event—you categorize it in the lower half of the purchase funnel—implementation will include activities such as invitations to qualified attendees, product interactions and "experiential" opportunities such as test drives and hands-on demonstrations. Clearly, the greatest "bang for the buck" is offered by events geared to the bottom half of the purchase funnel. Events are perfect for this because they can provide the kind of compelling emotional interaction with the product that drives sales.

Step 4 — Measuring results

To determine if the event has met its objectives, a metric plan and supporting tactics will be designed into the program to provide the necessary feedback and analysis. As I've mentioned, these metrics can include everything from consumer surveys to media impressions to incentive redemptions and sales. Again, it depends on the objective of the event and where it falls in the purchase funnel.

Of course, this is a very streamlined template. As with most complex endeavors, the devil is in the event details. The next few chapters look at how the cosmic spiderweb comes together now that the right people have been put into play and the event has been planned in conjunction with the overall marketing strategy.

Another way to look at this process is by examining the graphic on page 99. This loop represents the *event-specific implementation process*. It starts at **Stage 1** at the top by identifying the customers and determining their expectations. Also during this time, the core team identifies the processes, measurables, and roles and responsibilities of each team member. This stage also includes assigning of the project owner, who is responsible for keeping the event on track by coordinating all internal and external activities, and by developing administrative procedures and tracking reports.

Stage 2 kicks off with a start-of-work meeting of the core team to further define event specifics, objectives and requirements. The group also adopts standard tools at this juncture to track program progress.

Stage 3 basically encompasses the implementation of the processes. During this implementation period, the core team meets regularly to review processes and measurables.

Stage 4 involves an analysis of customer feedback, usually in the form of survey results, but through other measurement tools as well, to determine how successfully the event met expectations. Based on this analysis, future events can be continuously improved.

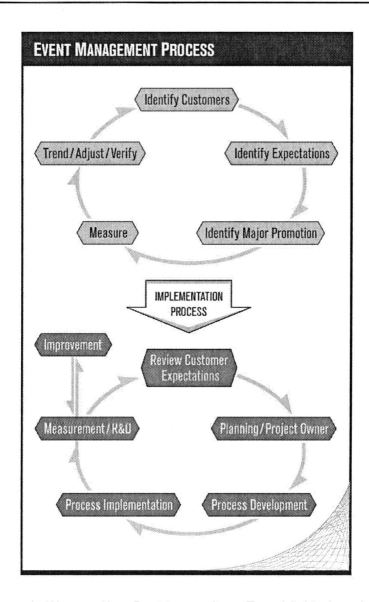

EVENT MANAGEMENT PROCESS

Identify Customers

Trend / Adjust / Verify

Identify Expectations

Measure

Identify Major Promotion

IMPLEMENTATION PROCESS

Improvement

Review Customer Expectations

Measurement / R&D

Planning / Project Owner

Process Implementation

Process Development

All events should be managed by an Event Management Process. The top half of the diagram above shows the overall process that can be implemented for nearly all events to ensure that they align with overall brand strategies. The first step is identifying the customer, followed by identifying customer expectations. Processes in support of the event can then be developed to ensure that the event meets customer expectations. These processes are then measured against customer expectations and continually improved as necessary. The bottom half of the diagram shows the process used for implementing a specific event.

The key criteria for a successful event

You can maximize the potential for an event's success by fulfilling three basic criteria:

1. *Identify and select a qualified audience.* "Qualified" in this reference means several things. It means that your audience fits into an economic demographic appropriate to your product. It also means that they are in the market, that is, ready to buy. You may have an audience of people who are *financially* equipped to buy Cadillacs, but if they've all just recently purchased new vehicles, they aren't as qualified as people who own older vehicles and are getting ready to buy new ones. Qualified also means *appropriate* in terms of lifestyle preferences.

2. *Identify a destination venue.* The site for the event should be someplace that your qualified audience has made a decision to attend, either because they've been invited or because they are attracted by the passion points being emphasized. You shouldn't hope or assume that your prospective customers will just happen to be walking by your event and might stop in.

3. *Create an interactive experience.* In addition to providing a more dynamic environment, interactivity intensifies the customer's emotional bonding with the product. Customers have come to expect this interaction. Anything less and you will not have captured their imaginations. You will not have moved them to a greater level of consideration.

> *When your event concentrates on these three criteria,*
> *the potential for sales increases tremendously.*

With the event planning accomplished, it's time to get into the real "nuts and bolts" of event marketing, which constitutes not only the next chapter on logistics but also the remaining chapters of this book.

"Budget is power."

Event marketing requires tremendous  resources, not only in terms of talent, time and effort by human beings, but also for the "hardware" of an event— the displays and exhibits, structures and modifications, printed materials and website development. Then there are costs such as transportation, communications, rental fees, licenses, agency fees and scores of other services. Throw in costs for customer surveys—just for "good measure"—and you can see why, even though you have the finances to host an event, budget rules.

Case Study:
Bud Light teams up with the Ironman

I'm indebted to Mitch Meyers, a true visionary in the area of sponsorships, for this case study, in which she was closely involved.

With Miller Lite having previously established itself as the predominant light beer in the American market, Anheuser-Busch had an uphill struggle on its hands when it rolled out its Bud Light brand in 1982. So it was fitting that Bud Light seized the opportunity to sponsor the not-well-known-at-the-time Ironman Triathlon, which had been taking place annually for five years on the Big Island of Hawaii. At the time, few people had even heard of a triathlon, which included a 2.4-mile swim, a 112-mile bicycle race and culminated in a full, 26.2-mile marathon. All in the space of less than half a day.

Beer products had long been associated with professional sports (remember the former pro athletes in all those Miller Lite commercials?), but full ownership of an event like the Ironman Triathlon was a novelty, and, at first, it perhaps seemed a little strange. Associating beer with paunchy middle-aged ex-football players was one thing, but beer and world-class marathoners? That was new.

But it also made sense. The Bud Light brand was after a more youthful market than the Budweiser market, people who wanted to look fit and be active. And the Ironman Triathlon epitomized fitness and health. And, of course, a big thing the night before the event was carbo-loading, and Bud Light fit right into that. Bud Light eventually helped expand the original event by sponsoring "mini" Ironman Triathlons in other major markets across the United States.

Another goal was to develop some loyalty within the sport itself. No other sponsors were putting money behind the event, and by owning the sponsorship, Bud Light could bring in other cosponsors, which eventually helped put the sport on the map. By creating this loyalty at the grass roots level among participants and aficionados, Bud Light began to develop a core group of influencers that helped to establish the brand quicker than might have happened by relying on traditional advertising.

Chapter Checklist

Checklist

- Event marketing is definitely a team endeavor, requiring an effective leader and team members who bring specific experience and expertise.

- Team leader attributes include: the ability to see the "big picture," but also to be detail-oriented; the ability to recognize and effectively utilize talent; a flair for the offbeat; a keen awareness of popular culture; and the willingness to suppress his or her ego to the event itself.

- The core team—those experts whom the team leader assembles to make the event happen—should include:
  - The program manager
  - Design experts
  - The financial person
  - Public relations counsel
  - Advertising experts
  - Legal advisors
  - Experts in research and measurement
  - Logistics experts
  - Website designers

- The event-specific implementation process is a four-stage progression that describes the functional steps in the event lifecycle.

–Step 1: Identify customers, processes, measurables and responsibilities.

–Step 2: Start-of-Work meeting to further define event specifics.

–Step 3: Event implementation.

–Step 4: Analysis of customer feedback data and event refinement.

Chapter 5
Logistics

"Never confuse movement with action."

— Ernest Hemingway, American author

The Cosmic Spiderweb

The *Random House Webster's* dictionary defines logistics as "1. the branch of military science dealing with the procurement of equipment, movement of personnel, provision of facilities, etc. 2. the planning, implementation, and coordination of the details of any operation." The word derives from the French term for lodging, as in the quartering of troops. To me the word means, Did the trucks with all the displays get to the location on time?, or, Are all the vehicles at the driving courses gassed, and fully prepped before consumers start driving them? Or countless other details that need to be identified or implemented in the "web" of activities surrounding any event.

Nevertheless, having planned and implemented hundreds of marketing events, I would have to say that the fact that logistics derives from a military term is appropriate. Holding events often seems as complex and complicated as prosecuting a military campaign. For the purposes of event marketing, however, logistics refers to the competency that obtains and supplies the resources necessary for the implementation of an event. It covers everything from site selection to transportation. It also involves the "nuts and bolts" capabilities—working with vendors and suppliers, maintaining security, procuring of structures and displays—in other words, making sure that things are where they are supposed to be when they are supposed to be there. Logistics sounds unglamorous compared to the excitement and creativity involved in developing and planning an event, but without effective logistics, any event is almost certain to fail. Logistics encompasses a complex range of activities, but most of these activities fall into one or more of the categories below. Keep in mind that a good deal of overlap is involved; it's a good idea to confirm responsibilities during the planning stages of the event so that everyone is clear on his or her duties.

Site selection

Obviously, an event has to take place somewhere in space. The choices are numerous and are usually determined by the size and type of the event you have planned. Marketing events often utilize convention centers and exposition halls. These venues are hardwired to accommodate events such as auto shows and similar, traditionally more static types of events. The obvious advantage of indoor locations like these is that the weather is basically neutralized. In addition, vehicle access patterns, parking and pedestrian traffic flow are pretty much established. Labor is often supplied by the host community, and a stable of vendors and suppliers has established a relationship with these venues. You basically have a turnkey situation in which you show up with your displays and exhibits, assemble them and plug them in.

I'm making it sound a lot easier than it is, of course. Even with venues that are accustomed to the rigors of event management and implementation, glitches and complications arise. In addition, with established venues, you'll be competing with other organizations for the space. Often, exposition halls and other indoor venues are scheduled well into the future. And you're pretty much restricted by the size and configuration of the venue. That's not usually a problem for events where customer participation and interaction is minimal.

But, as I have already pointed out, the new event paradigm places a premium on the customer's experiential encounter with the product. And let's face it, if your product is an automobile, it's hard to offer test drives within the confines of an exhibit hall.

Outdoor "greenfield" locations

A major trend in event marketing is the product immersion opportunities offered by happenings such as the Sturgis Rally and customer loyalty events such as Camp Jeep and the GM Saturn reunions in Springhill, Tennessee. These events feature a wide variety of activities and play host to thousands of people. They aren't the kind of things you can host in convention centers. In effect, events like these entertain groups the size of respectable municipalities, and in many cases, all of the needs of a small town are replicated in the event. It's a big job and it calls for specialized help from experienced organizations.

These organizations, which are relatively new in their specialization, are called event management and logistics companies. Usually this includes site management as well. These companies assist in selecting, designing, procuring and managing the site.

Location, location, location

The first consideration that goes into the selection of a site has to do with the overall marketing strategy and objectives you define to accomplish that strategy. If the objective is the "lower funnel" experiential opportunity for customers described above, your site will need to be large enough and accessible enough to accommodate the experience you have in mind. If this means off-

"Hide the wires."

Logistics for an event entails a complex and complicated series of activities that must be minutely planned and coordinated to ensure success. It obviously involves management at the 30,000-foot level. But the mystique of all this exquisitely choreographed activity can be blown if attention to detail is overlooked. My suppliers know that I am famous during pre-event walk-throughs for spotting visible cords and wires. This isn't just a matter of nitpicking. I equate it to spotting a cockroach in a five-star restaurant; seeing the cockroach doesn't necessarily diminish the restaurant's quality, but it sure does send the wrong signals to patrons.

road test drives, for example, you're talking about some significant acreage in a relatively unpopulated area with some particular terrain specifications.

Accommodations

Assuming that at least some of your staff and attendees will be flying to your event, it makes sense to locate it as close to an airport as is convenient. Failing that, a system should be set up to transport attendees from the airport as conveniently as possible, perhaps using a shuttle system. If your event is a multi-day affair, people will have to secure lodging. You'll need to make sure that there are enough hotel or motel rooms in the area to accommodate your attendees. Alternatively, if you intend to house the attendees on-site, you'll need to make provision for that. Does the site provide enough area for parking? Are there amenities nearby such as food markets, pharmacies, auto service facilities and convenience stores? Are medical facilities close enough to handle the sick or injured if necessary? Also, since one of the objectives of your event is likely to be media coverage, is the location close enough to a significant media market to make it worth the trip for reporters and camera crews? Is the event close enough, for example, for a radio station to do a remote broadcast from your event?

Accessibility

How accessible is the site to interstates and other major roads? If you'll be running thousands of visitor vehicles in on one-lane highways, you're probably going to be causing some traffic headaches for people you really don't want to alienate. You're also likely to irritate the people you most want to have embrace your product—your customers. Most of these folks are prepared to endure some inconvenience, perhaps, but they aren't usually looking to relive Woodstock. Traffic bottlenecks also complicate logistical issues such as the transportation and delivery of displays and exhibits. The transportation requirements for Route 2003, for example, call for close to 30 semitrailers for freight and display automobiles—the caravan of vehicles for this program would be more than half a mile long end-to-end. Obviously, room for parking, maneuvering, and loading and unloading these vehicles needs to be taken into account. And, the site needs to anticipate evacuation plans, and fire, police and emergency contingencies.

Scheduling

Depending on the type and size of event being planned, as many as a hundred trucks or more could be required to transport things like exhibits, displays, tents, tables and chairs, food, computers and other electronic equipment, structures (sound stage and equipment), office and talent trailers, Port-a-Johns, wood chips for walking paths, medical supplies and other freight. That's a lot of material and it can't all arrive at the same time because it would overwhelm the manpower available to unload and set it up where required. Therefore, the logistics team needs to stagger these arrivals, yet make sure that they all arrive and are appropriately dealt with. This can be a huge timing issue, especially when weather, breakdowns and other delays can complicate delivery schedules.

Weather

What about climate and weather? Is the area you've selected subject to severe weather conditions? I'm not just talking about thunderstorms, but also snow emergencies, flash floods, spring tornadoes and wildfires. If so, perhaps a venue with less volatile climate would be a better choice. Does the local community have the capability to deal with severe weather conditions should they arise? It's also important to identify other weather capabilities that can be used during your event. Local law enforcement authorities, aviation centers and TV weather channels all can provide information to be assimilated during the decision-making process.

Modifications

Often for major events, some reconfiguration of the terrain is necessary. For Jeep 101 events, we actually build an off-road course that includes a steep hill, dirt roads of various surface conditions, natural-banked curves and other features. How easy is that going to be at the site you've selected? Perhaps more important for good relationships with the local host community, how easy will land reclamation efforts be? Can you get heavy equipment into the area easily? Are there environmentally sensitive areas that need to be taken into consideration? What other kinds of restrictions might there be on the use of the

Staging area for the transportation of vehicles, display properties and signage as part of the Route 2003 tour.

land? As you can see, site selection involves a lot more than just picking out an empty parcel of land and pitching your tents on it.

Site surveys

Once a general location has been identified, the event management and logistics team will go out on site surveys to reconnoiter the specific location. This includes everything from helicopter photography to physically walking the site. Then they will negotiate with the owners for the rental of the property. They'll also secure the necessary permits and will liaison with the local administrative entities, such as the fire and police departments and waste management authorities. The event management and logistics team will also handle insurance for the event.

Site design

Only after all these requirements have been taken care of does the site management and logistic firm begin to design the layout of the site. This is why the event management and logistics firm usually sits in on the planning meetings. Designing a large event site from scratch can be as complicated as designing a small village, and most of the municipal functions of a village or town are the responsibility of the logistics firm as it configures the site. For example, large events on greenfield sites require tremendous power, which typically means the importation of massive generators. These need to be placed as inconspicuously as possible. Pedestrian traffic flow has to be engineered to maximize the positioning of displays and exhibits. Tents have to be placed strategically, as do off-road courses and other activity arenas. Where will the entertainment take place and how can interference and distractions from other activities be minimized?

Not least of the considerations is the placement of comfort stations and lavatory facilities. You may need to have an emergency medical station, not to mention evacuation routes and easy access for emergency vehicles. And what about food? Where do you want people to concentrate their eating in relation to everything else that's going on and how will you allow for effective trash disposal?

Staffing

While it would seem that the endless details, the pinpoint scheduling and the physical challenges of moving, installing and maintaining event components would be the greatest challenge of logistics people, it's not the case. "The job is the easy part," says Richard Tarzian of ICC, a major event logistics company. "It's keeping all the personalities in check. If anything, it's more of a staffing issue."

Traveling events, especially, need to have crews that sustain some continuity from venue to venue. It makes for efficiencies in unloading and setup, breakdown and loading, the rhythm of the traveling event. Even the exact sequence of what gets loaded first is important to repeat time after time. To have to hire new people in each location would destroy these efficiencies and hopelessly disrupt schedules. But those are all fundamental steps, according to Tarzian.

"It's the real-life road rules—like the MTV show—that's a challenge. Our people are traveling together. Sometimes we have a staff of more than a hundred. We take over entire floors of hotel rooms. Sometimes that can overwhelm a hotel. I've been a best man at weddings of people who have worked for me, a godfather to their children, and, unfortunately, I've witnessed a couple of divorces as well. All the same real-life experiences that people have in their normal lives they have on the road with us as well."

And the road is literally what it is. When a large traveling event is packed up in semis and ready to head for the next location, the entire crew travels via surface vehicles as well. "The logistics of trying to fly people to the next site would be a logistical nightmare," says Tarzian. So, essentially, the event becomes a caravan.

Catering

A key logistics responsibility is providing for catering. The logistics company identifies the caterers, selects the menu, picks the beverages, rents the chairs and tables and whatever cooking devices need to be used. Here again, it is important for the logistics company to understand the lifestyle preferences of the attendees. Some groups will appreciate a buffet of fried chicken and other "meat and potatoes" menus, whereas other groups would be more comfortable with a "sit-down" style with an entirely different menu. Special dietary requests need to be determined and honored. When the meal is over, the bill has to be paid and the area has to be cleaned up. And all this has to happen like clockwork.

The issue of food brings up other issues as well, such as requiring refrigeration—i.e. plenty of ice in warm weather—to keep the food fresh. Each state health department has its own requirements and standards with regard to the transporting, storing, handling, preparation and serving of food in public venues. Some health departments like to have their inspectors on-site while others take a more "hands off" approach. But all states take their responsibility for safeguarding the public health seriously, and your caterer and others involved in the provision of food and refreshments will need to work closely with the state health agencies to ensure a smooth operation.

Other responsibilities of the logistics team

Sometimes the list can seem truly endless. Logistics companies can coordinate with as many as 60 vendors for one event. Following are some of the tasks that seem invisible but come about as a result of the effectiveness of the logistics team. Where possible, the logistics team will use local companies and resources for these activities:

- Negotiation of site fees
- Negotiations with vendors, suppliers, unions, etc.
- Installation of phone lines
- Setup of tents
- Rest rooms, comfort stations
- Setup of displays and exhibits
- Staffing of the event
- Transportation
- Loading and unloading
- Electrical
- Air conditioning
- Procurement and installation of sound systems
- Satellite TV truck hookups
- Pathway construction
- Fencing erection
- Landscaping
- Coordination with stage companies
- Tables, chairs and bleachers
- Potable water
- Insect control
- Dust suppression
- Waste water disposal
- Environmental reclamation

Lou Bitonti

Dealing with the local communities

A major event can draw 50,000 people or more. That means lots of commotion and disruption to the local community, especially if they're not used to it. Typically, local residents recoil from the idea of an event in their community. It can mean upheaval to their daily routines, including increased traffic, more noise, a heavier burden on local services and uncertainty about the impact on the environment and the population itself. Will the local crime rate go up? Will attendees "trash" the location? Most important, will the local quality of life improve or diminish as a result of the event?

Of course, the only real way to allay these fears is through the behavior of the event organizers and the attendees. Relationship-building with the local community, through regular communications, through the purchasing of local goods and services, and through respect for local customs and property, is critical to a successful event. Jay Gordinier of Gordinier & Associates, Inc., an event management and logistics firm, points out that a good guide is to follow the SEEE plan. "SEEE stands for events that are concerned with Safety, Education, Entertainment and the Environment. Stressing these major components of the event helps local residents to understand the positive intentions of event planners," says Gordinier. "It's all about developing relationships."

As you can "see," the complexity of event site design calls for significant experience and preparation. And we haven't even yet discussed what has become one of the major issues of event planning.

Security

September 11, 2001, was a watershed day in our nation's history. Homeland security assumed unprecedented priority. Suddenly, our collective vulnerability to terrorist attack caused us to reevaluate everything from the safety of air travel to the security of our borders to the very integrity of our postal system. Today, it is a rare public event that does not require the inspection of packages or the use of metal detectors. It's an unfortunate fact of modern life that the collection of large groups of people in one place, which is the goal of most events, can be a temptation to people with terror on their minds. Just think back to the 1996 Olympics in Atlanta and the havoc and damage created by one lone bomber. Given the nature of marketing events, security has to be an integral part of event planning.

Ideally, security is effective but unobtrusive. But while that's a commendable goal, the reality is, security in the post-9/11 world is more visible than ever. That's not necessarily a bad thing. Highly visible security can provide a sense of reassurance. Nevertheless, since the positive customer experience is the ultimate goal of most events, security shouldn't be left to amateurs.

In some locations, it's often possible to utilize members of local law enforcement to implement security. This approach has significant advantages. Local law enforcement obviously has local intelligence. The local police know who the area troublemakers and security threats are. They also have jurisdiction and authority on their side. In addition, using local resources—not just police, fire and medical personnel—but local merchants, suppliers and vendors—helps forge good relationships that can only improve the event experience for your team and your customers. Of course, if the local law enforcement contingent cannot provide sufficient manpower, it will be necessary to hire additional security personnel. It is extremely important that security firms be researched carefully. Remember, their attitudes and behavior will reflect on your organization. They need to be professional and competent, not just "muscle." Remember what happened when the Rolling Stones hired members of the Hell's Angels for security at their free concert in Altamont? Nobody is likely to make that mistake again. Still, getting references on your candidates for security is a good idea.

Assuming you do have a good security team in place, what should your security strategy be?

To determine that, your first step should be a threat assessment. This process will look at the range of occurrences that could present a risk to people and property. A little later we'll talk about an even more comprehensive assessment in the discussion of the crisis-management process, and, in fact, the threat assessment might very well be contained in the overall crisis-management program. But for purposes of security strategies, we'll break out the threat assessment.

The threat assessment looks primarily at man-made crises such as acts of terrorism and other forms of violence such as fights and riots. It also includes a look at your event's vulnerability to vandalism and property destruction and other criminal behavior such as theft, and nuisance issues such as disturbing the peace, inappropriate public behavior—even animal control. Again, the goal is to make the experience as positive as possible for the attendees, so the more disruptions to that positive experience you can anticipate, the better you will be prepared to deal with them. The threat assessment should be a joint effort with the security component—including local law enforcement whether or not they are part of that component—along with the event program manager and site manager.

Once the potential threats are identified, contingency plans should be developed to address each one so that everybody will know their roles in the event of a threat burgeoning into reality. This means, at the very least, that people will know whom to contact and that the frontline security force will have a game plan for responding to the threat. For example, in the case of a release of a hazardous biological or chemical substance, are the local police and emergency agencies equipped to deal with the fallout? Is a bomb squad available? Can the local fire department adequately respond to a fire as a result of arson? Are the local police trained in crowd control? It's regrettable that we have to take these potential disasters into consideration, but it's also an unfortunate reality.

Event Marketer magazine offers some additional tips for event security:

- **Crowd dynamics**—Anticipate them. Know your attendees and what they might be capable of.

- **Site survey**—"Get an idea of where consumers will be, and where problems may arise."

- **Quantity of security staff**—Don't overload it, but certainly don't understaff.

- **Quality of security staff**—Professional law enforcement officers will have training, but will they have experience in events (how to safely restrain attendees, nonviolent crisis intervention, tactical communications, dispute resolution, etc.)?

- **Staff equipment**—Will security carry firearms? What about pepper spray or batons? At the least, they should have two-way radios with ear pieces.

- **The uniform**—"Problems tend to repel from uniforms." *Event Marketer* recommends avoiding T-shirts emblazoned with the word *security*, because it evokes the image of bouncers.

- **Pre-event briefing**—Reconfirm responsibilities, assignments and functions.

- **Staff hierarchy**—Monitors the security team's effectiveness.

- **Communications**—Frequent and regular reporting is essential to a coordinated security effort.

- **Spread the word**—Let attendees know the ground rules. Make sure they know if campfires are illegal or noise levels need to be kept down. If alcohol is forbidden, attendees should know it in advance.

- **At the entrance**—Use metal detectors if available and search all bags. There was a time when attendees might have resented these intrusions, but that time was before 9/11.

- **The crowd**—Be alert for flashpoints—threatening body language, menacing group behaviors, and, well, people who are behaving suspiciously.

- **The escort**—If it becomes necessary to eject someone from the event, ask them to leave voluntarily. If they refuse, escort them out as quickly and as professionally as possible. A well-trained security team should know how to do this with as little drama as possible.

- **Holding area**—"Create a detainment area, a room where ejected attendees can be held for local police."

- **Medic alert**—Make sure enough medical technicians are on call. Plug them into the communications network.

- **The finale**—Get security moving into wrap-up mode well in advance of the end of the event. Control traffic at exits to prevent mishaps.

- **Post-event report**—"Should be created with 24 hours. Must include a log detailing all situations and events, key mistakes and learnings and a recommendation for improvement."

Checklist

- Logistics encompasses a complex range of activities related to obtaining and supplying the resources for an event and for its actual implementation.

- Specific logistics involve a wide spectrum of activities and responsibilities including:

  –Site selection

  –Scheduling

  –Site surveys and site design

  –Staffing

  –Catering

  –Traffic

  –Electrical

  –Waste management

  –Parking

  –Accommodations

  –Negotiations with vendors and suppliers, local authorities

  –Transportation

  –Security

  –And myriad others

Chapter 6
Eye Candy

"The medium is the message."

— Marshall McLuhan,
Canadian communications theorist

What's that inflatable gorilla all about?

Eye candy. At its most unsophisticated level, you have those huge inflatable gorillas. You've seen them. A store has a grand opening and they rent a 40-foot-tall gorilla and perch it on top of their new building. Sometimes auto dealerships rent them for sales events. Why not? They attract attention, right? Like I said, that's at the most unsophisticated level. The point is, people respond to visual attractions. In the case of the giant inflatable gorilla, the response might be, "What does a giant inflatable gorilla have to do with cars, or a sale at Home Depot or the grand opening of a new CVS?" I don't exactly know how many people, upon seeing one of those huge snarling creatures looming on the horizon as they go about their Saturday afternoon errands, suddenly point the car in the direction of the gorilla to find out what it's all about. I suspect not too many. Probably as many people are offended by the sight as are attracted to it. And most of those who are offended are probably offended because the gorilla insults their sense of congruity. That gorilla might work for a toy store opening, or the premiere of a King Kong movie, but for just about anything else, it's so incongruous as to be ridiculous.

Visual congruity

As experiential phenomena, marketing events appeal to the senses. But the sense that predominates is the visual. Of course, there are other sensory experiences. Entertainment can appeal to the auditory as well as the visual sense. The ability of consumers to get a visceral, tactile sense of products during activities such as off-road test drives offers another sensory avenue. Even the smells and tastes of food appeal to the senses. Nevertheless, it is the visual attraction—the eye candy—that creates the most powerful impression for most people, at least initially.

Typically, the first appeal of an event is to the eye. Signage, displays, exhibits—all of them appeal to the visual and serve to invite the attendee into the experience. Visual stimulation attracts and compels. It may not be the direct inducement to the sale, but it is essential to drawing the customers in. Again, to return to the spiderweb analogy, it is the visual beauty of the structure that attracts "visitors" to the spider's web.

Of course, spectacular visual effects are not new. P. T. Barnum relied on the visually unusual and bizarre to attract customers to his shows. Walt Disney's first medium was the animated film, which he turned into colorful, three-dimensional exhibits and life-size characters for Disneyland and, later, Disney World. In *The Experience Economy*, Pine and Gilmore make the case that the new experiential economy is essentially theater, and what is theater but primarily a visual medium?

What *is* new is the way in which visual elements are now integrated into the theme of the event, which, in turn, reflects the underlying marketing strategy and objectives. Visual aspects of event marketing, if they are designed correctly and used effectively, are not mere ornaments. Rather, the displays and exhibits support and reinforce the marketing message, further intensifying the emotional experience for the customer.

The use of architecture is the fundamental starting point to the event experience. Whether it be smooth-flowing shapes that speak to aerodynamics and a sense of flow, large, bold columns and walls that produce a sense of stability and strength, or sharp angles and metals that provide an "edgy," "in motion" feeling, it all begins here. Add to that the application of color and texture through the use of finished materials, and the desired emotional response starts to take shape.

Anyone who has studied art knows the dramatic impact that color has on the subconscious mind. Careful thought should be given when selecting a color theme as you are impacting emotion here. Another important factor to take into account is the way color is interpreted differently throughout the world. In the same way that it's important to know how simple body language or gestures are interpreted in the international arena, so it is with color. A color that may invoke a positive response in many areas of the world may create a negative response in others.

The visual elements of an event tap into the emotions by connecting with the customers' passion points—those lifestyle preferences that customers use to define their values and beliefs. Visual effects are carefully orchestrated to harmonize with the psychology of the customers. In other words, if the displays and exhibits are effective, they will be impactful, yes, but also *familiar* in a way. Customers will feel as though they are in their element, not like strangers in a sterile showroom or market. Customers in such environments feel less pressure, more informed, more in control of the transactional process, and, therefore, more inclined to buy.

Next, you need to weave in the messages that are important to achieve your goals and objectives. If you are truly creating the experience, you must satisfy your mind on all levels of awareness. You have already set the tone with the architecture that created the mindset with the shape. The colors and

131

textures send a more subtle message to the mind, reinforcing the mood and emotion of the environment. Now, it is important to supply the brain with the more straightforward messages you want the customers to take away with them. Proper messaging should be a tiered structure. It begins with the broad stroke message such as capabilities, "global reach" or "quality" standards and ultimately narrows down to the specific product or service that you intend to deliver, the latter being the straightforward conscious message that you set out to communicate.

In addition to creating a receptive atmosphere, visual stimuli help to make events memorable, a hallmark of the experiential marketing phenomenon. As Pine and Gilmore point out: "Buyers of experience . . . value being engaged by what the company reveals over a duration of time. Just as many people cut back on goods to spend more money on services, now they also scrutinize the time and money they spend on services to make way for more memorable—and more highly valued—experiences."

Signage and graphics — The messaging tool

But a positive experience begins long before your customer ever sets out to go to the event. If your goal is a targeted audience, then visual stimuli frequently first appear in the form of an invitation or introduction to the event. Here is your first chance to set the expectation of what's to come, your first piece of eye candy. Properly done, it will reinforce all of the drivers of your event. Whether it is a rugged outdoor theme or a refined luxury motif, it begins by setting the tone. Here it must be consciously understood what the event is about, when and where it is held, why customers should attend and what they can bring to the experience. However, the initial visual materials also set the subliminal bar as to the experience customers will have. Ideally there are a series of these "bar setters" leading up to the event.

Now it is time to go, and the experience begins. As we have all experienced, the commute to and the convenience of a location will affect our mood prior to arriving. Don't forget this factor in the site selection process; convenience is the key. Having already provided a map or directions in the invitation, the team must include signs along the way as the next step. To have your audience in the proper frame of mind is important to their ability to receive your experience and key messages. Having clear, readable and creative signage that is congruent with the theme is important. Properly placed directional signs along the way, access to parking and a clearly defined entrance all influence the mindset long before the focused experience begins.

Once customers arrive at the site, traffic flow is key to the tiered sensual inputs that it takes to communicate your message in an experiential manner. So often these preliminary "eye candy" elements are overlooked. As with any successful recipe, one or more missing ingredients, however small they may seem, ultimately affect the final outcome.

Decoration vs. engagement

If Pine and Gilmore are right about much of our economic activity being theater, then the setting of an event must be more than an afterthought. The atmosphere that provides the context for the event must be fully integrated into the event's purpose. Usually this means, once again, tapping into the passion points or lifestyle preferences of those whom you wish to attract to the event and reinforcing those preferences through sensory stimuli.

This also means that the visual element of an event, for example, must go beyond *decoration* to *engagement*. Something as innocuous as the choice of colors cannot be left to chance. Everything contributes to the total effect. At our Jeep 101 events, for example, we focused our visual displays on those lifestyle attributes and values that we have learned over the years are shared by current and prospective Jeep owners. These attributes include an outdoor orientation, a sense of ruggedness and adventure—the off-road mentality. Values include tradition, heritage and patriotism. After all, the history of the Jeep goes back to military roots and its reputation for durability and ruggedness in World War II. In fact, one of the most popular exhibits at Camp Jeep is the historical review chronicling the evolution of the Jeep brand, starting from its roots in World War II as the beloved vehicle of the American GI, through its transformation to civilian life.

But there are even more intangible values, like independence and self-reliance, which are powerful claims on a Jeep owner's loyalty. Therefore, the displays and exhibits supporting the Jeep 101 event reinforce these values. They appeal not to the country club set, for example, but to the rock climbers and white-water rafters—in other words, those who enjoy individual challenges and, usually, wide open spaces. It's a relatively young, active group that doesn't care much for guided tours.

Hence, the visuals include images of camping, hunting, fishing, hiking and other vigorous outdoor activities. The objective is to associate the product with the lifestyle in a way that makes the product almost appear to be a natural part of the landscape.

Creating an attractive space vs. creating an environment

While the event space must be enticing and congruent, it must also serve as a livable environment for the duration of the attendees' visit. Designers must create the signage to guide attendees through an event, and the signage must be thematically appropriate as well as informative. The signage, in turn, contributes to the flow of the event. It takes attendees through transition areas along a progression of exhibits and activities that makes sense in terms of a storyline. In fact, you can think of the various visual elements as illustrating a story, but in a vibrant, interactive, engaging way. Even an activity such as a rock wall, where attendees can test their climbing skills, is an illustration brought to life and an opportunity for interaction, an interaction that conforms to the lifestyle preference of the attendees, if the event manager has done his or her job. From an experiential point of view, it's an episode in the product immersion adventure.

Constructing reality: simulation and drama

Today's fabrication technology allows display houses to create environments and exhibits with extraordinary faithfulness to reality. If you've been to Epcot at Disney World and visited the World Showcase circuit, you know the level of detailed accuracy with which the technology can reproduce the look of another country. Similarly, eye candy for events can simulate geographical locations as well as geological formations. And when products are integrated into this simulated reality, the results can be very dramatic. Drama, in turn, appeals to the emotions. And as we've already discussed, the emotional connection between product and customer is the ultimate goal of the event marketing team.

Of course, the event's reality can be further enhanced by product displays. Obviously, the bigger and flashier the products, the more potential there is for this kind of enhancement. At our events for Chrysler, Dodge and Jeep, for example, specially produced, one-of-a-kind concept cars create tremendous excitement because of their bold designs and dramatic color schemes. They are like dashing prototype models come to life and ready to drive.

Props and décor

But eye candy doesn't refer only to the grand thematic event canvases. As with most things, attention to detail is what truly creates the emotional atmosphere of an event. The following is a list of some of these details:

- Lighting
- Table decorations
- Flowers
- Banners and flags
- Counters
- Kiosks
- Drapery and flooring
- Posters
- Backdrops and murals
- Stanchions
- Tents
- Balustrades, gates and other structures
- Cutouts
- Uniforms and costumes
- Printed materials

The key to assembling the details is to keep them consistent with the event theme, which essentially follows from the strategic objective of the event.

Formatting visual stimuli

As with an event itself, the visual stimuli that support it should have a logical progression. This formatting begins with an overwhelming first impression at the entrance of the event site that establishes a mood and evokes an immediate and powerful emotional response in the attendees. The stimuli then "levels out" or becomes somewhat more subdued in the event area proper, although it should subtly build to a crescendo, culminating in a surprise ending that leaves the guests with the desire for more. The last impression should be the most memorable, the one the attendees retain. An event, conference, or any effective meeting should follow this format.

Surprise

Surprise and the unusual are always the keys to creating a memorable event. Props and décor can lead a guest in one sensory direction and then change the direction with a different look. The element of surprise can also be created through props and décor by changing a stereotypical venue into something totally unexpected. Traditional décor elements can be exaggerated in size or in intensity of color to create a more lighthearted theme—almost a cartoon effect. An example of this is oversized blowup photos of cars with oversized tulips. In contrast to this exaggerated presentation, the more authentic the décor and look, the easier the perception.

Themed décor

Themed décor and props can be used to inform an event, tell a story, support a product, reinforce an era or destination or stimulate an emotion in a guest. Themed décor or props can be presented two-dimensionally, as in backdrops, flats or banners, even though they are painted in a way that suggests a three-dimensional appearance. Three-dimensional décor is more realistic and brings the guests into the event with different, and therefore more interesting, viewpoints.

Projecting visual images

With new, high-intensity projections, images can now be created in any size and in excellent detail for use as a stand-alone image or as a backdrop. The quality of these high resolution images is so good, they can even be projected on the sides of buildings. Even ceiling treatments can be created through projections. In other words, the visual images canvas that is the atmosphere of the event has expanded. And by changing projections, you can modify and expand on the theme of your event.

Lighting

Lighting is one of the most important elements of an event. Lighting can be designed to alter, enhance or dramatize the look of the décor or the theme of the event. In fact, our friendly giant gorilla on the building would be nothing at night without effective lighting. Lighting can create a hot look, a subtle look, a colorful, festive look, an elegant look, or an active, exciting look. Every emotion can be evoked through lighting. These different looks are created by the positioning of the lighting, the intensity of the lighting—even the color of lighting gels.

With motion lighting, images, perceptions and feelings can be manipulated during an event. You can use motion lighting to highlight different props at different times throughout the event, thereby changing the emphasis of the theme. Lighting can also eliminate unattractive areas of the venue and create different dimensions to the décor through the artful use of shadows. In addition, by raising and lowering lights, you can signal attendees to take certain actions. Light can also lend drama to activities like car entrances into an event, much as you would see in commercial shoots.

Utilizing lighting with scrims can create a "reveal" that gives a whole new look to an event, establishing the element of surprise. A scrim is a piece of cotton or linen fabric of open weave used as a drop or partition to create the illusion of a solid wall under certain lighting conditions or creating a semitransparent curtain when lit from behind. By lowering the intensity of the light in one area and raising it in another, the scrim can take on a different image.

Kiosks

Kiosks can be used not only to provide direction and supply (and collect) information but also to introduce the theme. Here the element of surprise leading up to the event can be developed. Kiosks can also lend consistency to the event through the use of logo repetition.

Draping and carpeting

The use of drapes and carpeting can both reveal and conceal. By adding color and texture, the fabric of drapes and floor coverings can underscore thematic elements of the event. Drapes can be used as backdrops for props or "directionals." Drapes can also be used as "reveals" providing for dramatic spatial effects. Drapes and carpeting can also conceal stains, imperfections, wires, unpleasant views and other things you don't want your attendees to see.

Centerpieces and table décor

Table centerpieces can personalize an event. They can be used to express and coordinate with the theme of the event, complement the menu, impose consistency as well as giving the tables individuality. Color plays a key role in the design of table décor (centerpieces and table treatments). And the texture of the décor can suggest the strength or subtlety of the theme. Centerpieces can be lit from underneath or from above. Lit by candlelight, centerpieces can project a warm, intimate effect; lit by pin spotting from above, the effect can be more dramatic. The flexibility of centerpieces even extends to their functionality. They can serve as dessert or they can double as giveaways, perhaps to match the event theme. The beauty of a completely dressed table with linens, base plates, candelabras and floral elements theatrically lit can complement the room.

Lou Bitonti

Costuming

By appropriately costuming the staff or by using costumed characters, you can further enrich your event's emotional value for attendees. The costumes can become another element of the décor, bringing it to life. Costumed staff and characters also add an element of interaction to the event and animate the theme. In many venues where space is limited, costumed characters can carry out the theme where the use of backdrops and three-dimensional décor might be restricted. If it is appropriate, you might also consider costuming for attendees. This draws them into the event, reinforces the thematic elements of the event and greatly increases the event's memorability. In essence, costumed guests become one with the event. This can be true even if the costume is no more than a hat, a scarf, or a T-shirt. As part of a larger agent event in Hawaii in the late 90s, Safeco Insurance Company took guests to a rodeo on one of the island's large cattle ranches. All the attendees received "10-gallon" cowboy hats and red bandanas, which, in addition to putting them into the rodeo mood, also created a sense of unity among the guests.

Cutouts

Life-size artist renderings of famous personalities and other unique individuals can personalize a party. These features can also create a sense of surprise, as when the renderings are of actual guests in costume scattered among the props and décor. Placement of the cutouts in front of backdrops can create a three-dimensional appearance, further bringing the space to life.

The palette available to today's event designers offers a wide range of possibilities for fulfilling the sensory expectations of attendees. The following case study illustrates how the creative use of eye candy can enhance the sensory experience while supporting marketing objectives.

Case Study: The Art of Driving

Challenge

DaimlerChrylser's objective with the Art of Driving event was to immerse owners and prospects into the new Chrysler brand image, an image that reflected upscale values such as sophistication, class, distinction and heritage. They also sought to use the platform of Art of Driving to launch the Pacifica and Crossfire models as part of the new brand image.

Specific objectives of the Art of Driving event included:

- Providing a complete brand immersion experience

- Identifying with the lifestyles of potential customers

- Increasing brand awareness and consideration among competitive prospects

- Building owner loyalty

- Generating qualified hand-raisers and driving them to the dealership

To accomplish these objectives, Creative Solutions Group, an event design firm, worked with DaimlerChrysler to identify key messages that aligned with the brand image. Together, they researched the attributes of the target audience (upscale, affluent) that best supported those key messages. Then they built activities and exhibits around these lifestyles to engage and entertain consumers, at the same time reinforcing the new Chrysler image as a premium brand associated with premium lifestyles.

Venues and environments

To create an atmosphere that suggested the lifestyle preferences of the target audience, DaimlerChrysler sought event sites that embodied the premium lifestyle. These included mansions, polo grounds and upscale golf courses. For example, one Art of Driving event was held just outside Detroit at Meadow Brook Hall, a former private residence often referred to as an "American castle." As the Meadow Brook Hall website states, "This magnificent 88,000-square-foot manor . . . beautifully exemplifies the lavish lifestyles and era of the American industrialists of the early 20th century." The 320-acre estate also hosts the annual Concours d'Elegance, showcasing rare classic luxury cars, all of which made it an ideal location for the Art of Driving event.

But identifying the Art of Driving event site was just the beginning. To sustain the ambiance of the event, the eye candy associated with it had to reflect the elegance of the site itself. Creative Solutions chose tent structures and shelters that had a certain design quality to them—chalet-style tents that one might see at a formal reception at an English country garden party. They also created a formal park atmosphere where you might find someone sitting on a park bench or strolling the grounds of an aristocratic estate. Elements of this

Meadow Brook Hall mansion in Rochester, Michigan, a site representative of the unique and upscale locations used for the Art of Driving events.

park atmosphere included, in addition to the park benches, appropriately designed light poles, premium landscapes and themed sculptures.

Displays and activities

To reinforce the brand image and capitalize on other marketing initiatives and events, the following event displays and activities were developed for the Art of Driving:

• *A launch/immersion tent* for the Pacifica and Crossfire that established the vehicles as the focus of the event and conveyed a sense of classic serenity and distinction through the use of spaciousness and open areas.

• *A Celine Dion concert theater tent* replicating the graceful lines of the coliseum dome at Caesar's Palace, with concert footage on a large screen in the theater. This display provided attendees with the sense of immediacy and excitement of being at the actual concert.

• *The Chrysler Heritage/Innovations exhibit* celebrating the rich history of Chrysler and looking ahead to the technology and innovations of the future. This exhibit included heritage displays depicting design inspirations through the decades (with a historic car photo op for guests); a display dedicated to the Chrysler-sponsored Heritage Racing series; a video to support brand messages; product quality displays and concept vehicles; technology and interactive displays such as a Pacifica cutaway and the Crossfire engine.

The lifestyle displays that supported the Art of Driving event focused on prestige and the "high life." These included:

• *The Grape & Grain* exhibit, sponsored by *Food & Wine* from American Express and featuring: a Kitchen Aide display; a *Food & Wine* "Best New Chef" cooking demonstration with food samples for guests; spring/summer beverages in keeping with the Art of Driving theme; a wine expert to

Entrance to the Art of Driving National Ride and Drive track.

The Art of Cooking tent at the Art of Driving Tour, sponsored
by *Food & Wine* magazine.

provide 15-minute tastings during the day and available to answer questions; magazine samples.

- *Body & Blend*, sponsored by Condé Nast Publications' *GQ* and *Details*. This exhibit was dedicated to the pleasures of fine cigars, with an authentic cigar roller furnishing complimentary cigars for attendees, educational discussions on cigars and a relaxing lounge where guests could enjoy a cigar at their leisure.

- *Form & Function*, sponsored by Hearst Magazines' *Esquire*, *Harper's Bazaar* and *House Beautiful*. This display area was devoted to style and interior design. It included a Fashion Area featuring a retrospective of design using magazine cover blowups to create a stunning fashion backdrop depicting the course of fashion through past generations. In addition, a Home Area—a staged "living room/great room" with furnishings—showcased the latest trends in home design, including the accoutrements of home entertaining such as a bar area and serving trays.

- *Live & Breathe*, sponsored by *W Magazine* from Condé Nast. This exhibit allowed guests to pamper themselves in style with an aromatherapy station, mini massages, liquid refreshments in the form of smoothies and water, and a sweepstakes with an opportunity to win a one-year spa membership.

- *Long & Short, sponsored by Callaway*. The exhibit focused on golf, a major passion point among members of the target audience. Included were two video swing analyzers with a follow-up email option if guests requested it, a custom-built putting green, Callaway golf product demos, custom club fitting, a Chrysler golf video monitor with tournament footage and highlights, Callaway golf apparel and accessories, an appearance by a Callaway Golf professional player, a Chrysler golf display and a golf history display.

- *Finally, the centerpiece of the Art of Driving, was,* in itself, an experience in the art of driving. Test tracks were created for both the Crossfire and Pacifica vehicles, as well as for other vehicles in the Chrysler line. Features of the test tracks allowed drivers to experience key attributes of the vehicles and included speed bumps, pot holes, head roll, acceleration and braking, and handling and cornering.

Ultimately, this unique event provided consumers with the complete experience of corporate and brand immersion, as well as firsthand knowledge through test drives (as many as 30,000) and competitive driving courses. It was supplemented with the lifestyle activities and historical perspectives represented for each brand/vehicle—a complete experience.

The Art of Driving event also provided DaimlerChrysler's Customer Relationship Management group with a tremendous opportunity to obtain specific demographic information and consumer preference data, especially in terms of response to product and corporate initiatives. As a result, DaimlerChrysler will be able to provide a smoother progression through the purchase funnel for the consumer, as well as continuing to build a qualified prospect event marketing database.

As I've suggested, eye candy can be a form of entertainment (the Celine Dion concert video footage used in the Art of Driving event is a good example of this). In the next chapter, we'll look at entertainment in its own right and how performance artists and other celebrities fit into the event mix.

A distinctive eye for layout and tent detail was used in implementing the
blueprint for the Art of Driving National Tour.

Chapter Checklist

Checklist

- Because "experiential" event marketing appeals to the senses for the emotional impact it is trying to achieve, the visual aspect of an event is of critical importance.

- Visual effects should be "congruent"—that is, they should support the themes and objectives of the event.

- Eye candy should create an engaging environment that is dramatic and stimulating.

- Specific elements of visual stimuli can include:
    - –Event venue
    - –Graphics
    - –Video
    - –Themed décor
    - –Lighting
    - –Draping and carpeting
    - –Exhibits

Chapter 7
Entertainment and Celebrities

"Pictures are for entertainment, messages should be delivered by Western Union."

— Samuel Goldwyn, Hollywood film producer

The Cosmic Spiderweb

Entertainment is actually quite a broad concept within the context of event marketing. It can encompass everything from the static, sensory enjoyment of one's surroundings to participation in exhilarating activities to celebrity "encounters" and full-blown concert experiences. In fact, the eye candy we discussed in the previous chapter is actually a form of entertainment because it elicits an emotional response to the display or exhibit or super graphic. And emotional responses are what entertainment is all about.

Entertainment is such an integral part of event marketing that it is often taken for granted, to the detriment of the event itself. That seems paradoxical. If entertainment is so central to events, how can it be detrimental? For the answer to that question, we have to go back to one of the primary tenets espoused in this book: Consumers today are looking for experiential relationships with products. They want that experience of the product to be memorable, and the event manager wants the memorable event to be positive. As I've pointed out, attendees to events respond most strongly—and positively—to those event stimuli that correspond most closely to their lifestyle preferences—their passion points, to use the advertising term.

Essentially, what that means is that people want to participate in events that reflect their lifestyle values. For example, those with an "outdoors" orientation—hunters, fishing enthusiasts, hikers, campers, rock climbers, etc.—sense an affinity with nature and the environment. Conversely, potential attendees at a home design and decorating show would exhibit lifestyle preferences more related to "home and hearth" issues. This isn't to say that your customers are conservative to the point of resisting something new. You always have to be innovating. But you have to innovate "within the white lines," to use a sports analogy. In other words, you can bring a football quarterback to a basketball game, but don't expect him to start draining three-pointers. And don't expect the fans to cheer.

If you're looking for celebrities to appear at each of the shows mentioned above, you might want somebody like Ted Nugent at the "outdoor" event and someone like remodeling veteran Bob Villa or Paige Davis of *Trading Spaces* fame at the "home" event. And you probably wouldn't want to get these three mixed up. The result would be a less than satisfactory experience for the attendees—and potential customers—at your event.

The point is, entertainers vary. They appeal to different audiences with different tastes and expectations. That should be a no-brainer, but it's amazing how many event marketing managers will sign on with an act or celebrity for his or her event having been blinded by star power or restricted by a budget or for whatever reason.

Eddie Haddad knows this paradox well. Haddad began as an entertainer himself and over the years has promoted some of the most memorable shows in the entertainment business, including the legendary 1984 Jacksons' Victory Tour and Marvin Gaye's final tour (The Midnight Love Tour). He has also managed some of the most famous names in the entertainment business, including Wayne Newton, the Isley Brothers and the O'Jays. Haddad also has a keen understanding of the psychology behind entertainment for event marketing. Says Haddad: "I believe that most of corporate America today has people working for them [in event marketing] that don't know the street, the heart of the public. They go by what's hot at the moment, whether or not the act will fit in well with their audience." And that, in a nutshell, is the fatal temptation: to assume that what's currently fashionable in entertainment will appeal to your audience simply by virtue of an act or entertainer's current popularity. You're basically falling victim to the "entertainment flavor of the week" syndrome.

Almost as bad is the marketing manager who makes decisions about booking a celebrity based on the personal preferences of the marketing manager, or the CEO or the CEO's wife, for that matter.

These approaches are deadly for a number of reasons.

Image is everything

Image is everything in business. Image creates brand value. And a product's image is a composite of many attributes, including the celebrities or entertainers that customers identify with your products. Just as the priority-one rule of the physicians' Hippocratic Oath is "First, do no harm," the first rule of entertainment, therefore, is to choose celebrities and entertainers that will not detract from your product's image or besmirch your company's reputation. Some choices will be clear-cut. Gangsta Rap acts probably won't contribute positively to the image of, say, disposable diapers, although we shouldn't be surprised if some ad agency, in the name of "creativity" somewhere comes up with just such a campaign.

However, almost as bad as doing outright harm is something we could call creating *incongruity*. Say, for example, as a marketing manager, you choose a celebrity spokesperson or an act that, while they aren't downright offensive, there is still some ambiguity. If the customer has to wonder what the connection is between your entertainment and your product, you've presented them with a disconnect. And that's almost as bad as an assault on your product's image. Again, this is the kind of thing that can happen when you go for

Lou's Laws

"Entertainment and celebrities are subordinate to the event."

The type of entertainment and celebrities you use for your event should be determined by the event's objectives. Therefore, decisions on entertainment and celebrities come later in the event management process. Avoid the temptation to be starstruck by who's available or who's "hot."

what's hot at the moment rather than what makes sense for your product and your market.

Not that you can anticipate everything, as the Dixie Chicks proved during the war with Iraq when they criticized President George Bush for his prosecution of the conflict. The Dixie Chicks are wildly successful and wildly popular. Up to that point, however, they hadn't been particularly political. But that's why it's so important to do your homework when it comes to selecting acts. The Dixie Chicks have every right to express their political views, even unpopular, controversial views. However, depending on your audience, you might not want to hear those views for the first time at an event for which you booked them as the entertainment.

Credibility

Bruce Willis driving a Jeep is credible. Arnold Schwarzenegger driving a Hummer is credible. Either of them driving a Mercedes would probably be credible as well, although the fit wouldn't be quite as appropriate to their cinematic images. (And now that Arnold is the Governor of California, I guess we could say that his being chauffeured in a limousine is credible, too.) But neither Bruce Willis nor Arnold Schwarzenegger is credible driving a Ford Focus.

That's a somewhat absurd example. But the point is, one way or another, the entertainment or celebrity you use to promote your product must be at least plausible as someone the public could envision using the product. Of course, if the celebrity actually *does* use the product—if Arnold tools around Hollywood in a Hummer, for example—so much the better in terms of credibility. Among companies that have made good choices recently in the use of celebrities to promote their products are Jaguar with Sting and Ford Truck with Alan Jackson.

Again, the main problem is that marketing managers will want to

Lou Bitonti

go for whoever's hot at the box office at the moment, reasoning that popularity equates with attention and will transfer to awareness and acceptance of their product. Unfortunately, it doesn't work that way, and lots of companies could save themselves a significant amount of money—not to mention credibility in the eyes of their customers—by avoiding that pitfall.

You *must* know your market. That means knowing the tastes and preferences of the individual consumers that make up your market. How do you do that? Often, you can do it by analyzing the data you've collected about your customers. Their age brackets, income levels, purchasing preferences, vacation habits and other attributes will give you an indication of the kinds of entertainment they gravitate to.

But, as Eddie Haddad suggests, there is only so much that you can ascertain about your customers through a reading of psychographic data. At some point, it becomes necessary to obtain "street level" intelligence on your customers. You need to communicate with them directly to learn about their

Kenny Loggins performing at the second Camp Jeep event, 1996, in the Rocky Mountains of Colorado.

enthusiasms and to understand the social and psychological dynamics that drive their preferences. In other words, you need to experience the "buzz" first-hand. This is especially true if you are trying to appeal to certain ethnic groups.

Negotiating agreements with celebrities

A typical celebrity agreement as it relates to an event has two components, reflecting the two basic uses of celebrities to promote products and services. The first half has to do with the name, likeness and image rights. In this component of the agreement, the celebrity grants to the client the right to use his or her name, likeness, image, voice, depiction, photograph, initials, testimonial, etc., for a price. Often, this entails a production day or several days to shoot a commercial, do some radio interviews or participate in a photo shoot. The other component of an agreement often deals with personal appearances. The celebrity will make himself or herself available to the advertiser for a certain number of days to personally appear at a trade show, event, special party, employee function or similar activity. Agreements with celebrities may entail either one or the other of these components. Nevertheless, for purposes of efficiency, the typical agreement contains both components. This is especially important in event marketing because the use of the celebrity's image is usually part of the effort to promote the event.

Does the celebrity have to use the product?

In the public imagination there is probably no more cynical human behavior than that regarding the celebrity product endorsement. If you were to line up a hundred people on the street and ask them if they thought Jason Alexander, for example, actually ate KFC chicken, a majority of this sample of consumers would probably say that they doubted it. Jason Alexander makes a lot of money, after all, and probably doesn't need to dine on fast food. But whether Alexander eats KFC or not is irrelevant. What matters is what the public *perceives.*

So, it might come as a surprise to some people that celebrity agreements typically don't *require* that the celebrity use the product. As I mentioned earlier with regard to credibility, it's really a matter of whether the public would find it plausible for the celebrity to be using a given product. Usually, when a celebrities connect with a product they have their own image in mind, and if they are getting the right advice, they'll usually pass on products that are incompatible with their image. In other words, it's not usually a problem. Most reputable agents will insist that their celebrities use the product in advance to be sure that they are comfortable with the product's quality. Having said this, many contracts stipulate that, since the celebrity is going to be affiliated with a certain product—say a car—the advertiser will supply the product to that celebrity with the understanding that the celebrity will use the product, perhaps not to the exclusion of all other similar products, but at least regularly.

Riders

Whether or not a celebrity is required to use your products might be something that's included on a *rider* to the contract. Indeed, the subject of the riders that entertainers require as part of their contractual agreement to perform or appear at events has become the stuff of legends. Event planners would do well to understand that some of these riders, especially what are known as "backstage riders," can be bizarre, indeed, not to mention costly. And these costs aren't usually included in the entertainers' fees. Backstage riders can include anything from requiring rooms to be painted a certain color to unusual requests for food to the really outlandish, such as Britney Spears' alleged demand that any incoming calls to the special phone in her dressing room (supplied by the purchaser of her services, of course) will result in a $5,000 fine to the purchaser. For more insight into this and some of the other "requests" made by celebrities, see The Smoking Gun website at www.smokinggun.com, which includes the backstage riders for numerous celebrities, including everything from a full-size snooker table for the Rolling Stones (they provide their own snooker billiard balls) to "1 medium serving bowl coctail [sic] franks in special sauce (consult with production assistant for the recipe and serving instructions)" for ZZ Top.

Should you use a celebrity?

As I've already suggested, the impulse to go for a celebrity as the cornerstone of an event is often a knee-jerk reaction. You can see why. We are a celebrity-obsessed culture. In the 30 or so years that *People* magazine has been around, it has spawned scores of imitators. The same is true of TV shows such as *Entertainment Tonight*. Awards shows on TV have proliferated not so much because the public clamors to see more awards handed out, but because it wants to see its celebrities on display. Watching Joan Rivers interview stars on the red carpet as they head for the Oscar ceremony has become mandatory viewing for many Americans in its own right, never mind the actual Oscar telecast. We have what seems to be an insatiable appetite for news about celebrities, and it doesn't appear to be diminishing.

The downside of this demand is that celebrities can charge big money for their services, and they do. *Event Marketer Online* recently provided a sampling of celebrity fees for a two-hour private show, according to Dallas-based National Booking Agency:

- Dixie Chicks: $1.5 million
- Kiss: $500,000
- Jennifer Lopez: $500,000
- James Taylor: $500,000
- Cristina Aguilera: $300,000

Of course, as I write this, these are some of the biggest names in show business. Not all celebrities can command fees in the six and seven figures range. But even lesser-known artists can charge as much as $50,000 or more for an appearance. All of which suggests that one of the first questions you need to ask yourself when considering the use of a celebrity for your event is, "Do I have the budget for it?" And the second questions is, "Can I get a return on this money at the end of the day?"

When asking yourself these questions, keep in mind that you can sometimes get a celebrity to do a special event appearance for a lower fee. For example, if the celebrity has an interest in a cause your event is promoting, he or she will often work for a reduced fee. Similarly, if a celebrity is not as busy as he or she would like to be, your event can provide much-needed visibility, for which, again, the celebrity might be willing to drop the price. (Of course, if the celebrity is looking for visibility, you have to ask yourself how valuable his or her fame is, unless the celebrity is in the "emerging talent" category.)

Lou with Sheryl Crow (middle) and Lou's wife, Christine, sharing a moment after Sheryl's performance at Camp Jeep, Vail, Colorado, 1997.

You also have the option of creative payment plans. Sometimes celebrities will take company stock (this was especially true in the mid-90s when Internet stocks were all the rage), or, depending on the product, you may be able to work out royalty deals in lieu of or in addition to a one-time lump sum fee.

How do you get to them?

Sometimes you can get to celebrities directly. More often than not, you need to approach them through their agent or representative. Depending on the celebrity, some use speakers bureaus, some have internal people who work within their own organizations. And if you're really uncertain about which celebrity would be right for your event, The Hollywood-Madison Group in Los Angeles can match your event up with the right star using its Fame Index celebrity database. According to an article by Keri O'Brien in *Special Events* magazine, the Fame Index database lists more than 10,000 celebrities, indicating their interests and charity affiliations.

Finally, it's important to remember that, in the old cliché, stars are people, too. How you approach celebrities and how you treat them can make a huge difference in their willingness to support your project and how they conduct themselves in that service. The following is an excerpt from an article by Rita Tateel, founder and president of The Celebrity Source, an international agency headquartered in Los Angeles that recruits and coordinates celebrities for corporate and nonprofit special events, public relations programs and product endorsement campaigns. The article is from *Special Events* magazine, and it offers tips on working with celebrities to help make the experience a positive one.

1. *Put yourself in a star's shoes and ask, "What's in it for me?"*

Before you ask a celebrity to participate in a project, PR campaign or special event, ask yourself this question if you were that celebrity: "What's in it for me; why should I do this?"

We all would like to think that celebrities get involved with cause-related events because they really care about the cause. While this can be a contributing reason (if they personally have been touched by the cause or have played a role in a film related to the cause), the truth is that most celebs are motivated by other factors.

If you have money, it's a great motivator. But when budgets are slim to none, great perks and gifts can go far in getting a celebrity to say yes.

Never underestimate the power of "S.W.A.G." (Stuff We All Get). There's a reason why the celebrity gifts for award nominees and presenters are so elaborate these days—some in excess of $20,000. There's a reason I always recommend that my clients include products or gifts as part of the celebrity request, even when celebrities are being paid. It's simple—celebrities are human beings like the rest of us, and everyone loves gifts.

The type of media exposure that can be gained through the event also may motivate celebrities to accept an invitation. However, be forewarned that those who are motivated by this the most include the up-and-coming and the down-and-going. There also are some celebrities who, because of personal circumstances in their lives, do not want to be exposed to the media. (Martha Stewart—need I say more?)

Other answers to the question "What's in it for me?" might include a celebrity's personal interest in the activity or sport, personal connections to the city, a desire to change one's image, the fun/exclusivity/prestige of the event, who else is involved, or simply who asked them.

2. *Make a list of everything the celebrity might want to know.*

Once a celebrity has agreed to participate, make a list of absolutely everything he or she might want to know and do—every question this personality might have—from arrival to departure. Then list all of your answers.

Celebrities and their representatives can become very demanding and difficult to work with if the celebrity feels insecure about his or her involvement. The best way to help make celebrities (and their representatives) feel secure is to demonstrate that you have considered every little detail and have anticipated their every question.

In my office, we imagine that we are the celebrity arriving at the event. We ask questions like, "What happens when I step out of the limousine? Who is going to greet me? If I'm running late, whom do I call, and how do I reach them? Will press be there as soon as I arrive? What happens next? With whom am I going to be seated? What exactly am I supposed to do? For how much time am I needed? Do I have to pay for my own drinks? Where are the bathrooms? How do I find my driver when I'm ready to leave?" etc.

Celebrity greeters or escorts should know the answers to every question the celebrity might have. If celebrities feel secure and trust that whoever is taking care of them will *really* take care of them, they will be much easier to work with.

3. *Respect their time.*

Time is a celebrity's most valuable commodity; don't waste it.

The bigger the celebrity, the less time he or she has. There are so many people wanting a piece of the celebrity's time, celebrities have to ensure that the time they do have to make an appearance is time well spent.

One timesaving strategy that celebrities really appreciate is limousine service to and from the event. This is not only convenient for the celebrities—they don't have to worry about traffic or parking—but it also gives them extra time to get some work done, make some important calls or study the briefing notes you sent them last week.

Limousines (which also can be sedans or SUVs with drivers) also are helpful to the event organizers. Thanks to cell phone communication with the driver, it's not necessary to stress over wondering whether the celebrity has gotten into the car yet, and it's helpful to know when the celebrity is five minutes away from arriving. It's also less likely that celebrities will cancel at the last minute when they know that a limousine is scheduled to pick them up. If, however, they do need to cancel, you'll know before the event, rather than wasting your time waiting around for someone who turns out to be a no-show.

Bottom line—make it easy for a celebrity to participate by offering limousine transportation, ask the celebrity for the minimum amount of time that will fill your needs, don't ask celebrities to arrive earlier than needed and *never* make them wait!

4. *Keep briefings brief.*

When a celebrity briefing session is necessary, determine whether it must be in person or if it can be handled by phone, fax or email. Of course, we all would rather meet celebrities in person. But remember my Tip No. 3—time is their most valuable commodity. So use phone, fax or email if you can.

If you must meet in person, have no more than one or two people at the briefing session, and make it as to the point as possible. More than an hour is seldom needed.

Celebrities won't want to memorize lots of facts and figures—unless they are being paid quite handsomely. Therefore, for briefing notes, I recommend no more than three to four bullet points of the most important information you want your celebrity to communicate to the media.

Fax or email briefing notes about a week in advance, and have a small cheat-sheet that you can hand to the celebrity on-site when he or she arrives—they will appreciate it. I've seen situations where the celebrity is talking to the media and has forgotten the name of the event or why they are there. This is not good for anyone concerned, including the celebrity.

5. *Don't make any promises you can't keep, and keep all of the promises you make.*

This business is so much about relationships (which is why, I suppose, after 15 years, people still return my phone calls). The quickest way to ruin a relationship with a celebrity or his or her representative is to not come through with something that was promised. That's why this is worth repeating: Don't make any promises you can't keep and keep all of the promises you make ... 'nuf said.

Activities as entertainment

As I've mentioned on several occasions, interactivity is a key to

Television crew interviews Lou as part of a nationally syndicated Camp Jeep TV show.

modern event marketing, and that applies to entertainment as much as to any component of the discipline. I've already alluded to the ride-and-drive opportunities at DaimlerChrylser product events. These can certainly be as entertaining as they are informative. But at almost any event marketing venue, you'll usually find a variety of activities in which attendees can participate. Examples of these activities include video games, golf swing analysis, bike courses for kids, soccer kicks, cooking demonstrations (with audience participation, of course), massage and other health and fitness therapies, fashion makeovers and fly casting clinics. And this list doesn't begin to exhaust all the possibilities. (For a more comprehensive list of event activities, see the Camp Jeep Case Study summary at the end of this book.)

Extending the entertainment factor beyond the event

Entertainment need not end with your event. You can extend the life of your event and reach a much larger audience through the creative use of video and television. To borrow a concept from the late Speaker of the House of Representatives, Tip O'Neill, all events are local. That is, they take place at a specific time and location. And without amplification from media of some sort, all events would *remain* local. Therefore, you could expect to impact only those people who actually attended your event. And, since the space of your location and the duration of your event are finite, there would be limitations to the number of people you could reach.

Because of its pervasive influence, television offers the greatest opportunity for "amplifying" your event. Eclipse Television & Sports Marketing, a firm that specializes in extending the life and excitement of events, understands very well how this process works. They have been turning local events such as "Jeep King of the Mountain" into national events for more than a decade. The King of the Mountain event, in fact, has been featured on the CBS, NBC and Fox Sports networks. I take pride in being one of the creators

Top downhill skiers at Jeep King of the Mountain with Lou (center).
From left: Franz Klammer, Austria, Olympic Gold Medal winner; Bill Johnson, USA,
Olympic Gold Medal winner; Pirmin Zurbriggen, Switzerland, Olympic Gold Medal
winner; Michael Veith, Germany, World Cup Champion; and Steve Podborski,
Canada, Olympic Bronze Medal winner.

of this competitive sporting event, which brings together teams of top professional and amateur skiers (including former Olympic competitors) and snow-
boarders in a unique race format that combines several popular downhill
events. It's an exciting event that brings together enthusiasts and participants
in a way that would otherwise be difficult to do, and it provides an excellent
showcase for the event's sponsors. However, as popular as the event is, without
television, its impact would probably not be worth the cost of holding it. But
introducing the event to a nationwide (and occasionally worldwide) television
audience completely changes the dynamic. Now, instead of several hundred
spectators and participants, you have millions. And just because someone does-
n't catch the show on TV doesn't mean he or she completely misses out on the
exposure to it. In the case of Jeep King of the Mountain, sports reports about the
event on TV, radio and in the newspapers further extend the coverage. Then
there are the special interest publications that cover skiing and other winter

sports. These outlets will usually run schedules and results if nothing else, and often they'll even get more in-depth with interviews and features on events such as Jeep King of the Mountain.

For Camp Jeep, we came up with a concept for extending the life of the event well beyond its actual scheduled days. We used actors who played the roles of family members visiting Camp Jeep (the "hero family"), and we recorded their activities for development into a "freestanding" program—a lifestyle special—that we could then market, or syndicate, to stations in local markets throughout the country. Using the concept of barter syndication, wherein program content is traded for an inventory of commercials (typically 50 percent), the cost of distribution is nearly 100 percent self-liquidating. What's more, Jeep is guaranteed a friendly context for its commercials. Most important, through this approach hundreds of thousands of viewers can experience the Camp Jeep phenomenon vicariously through the adventures of the "hero family" via a mainstream, network-quality TV production.

Entertainment is so integral to today's event marketing that it's impossible to think of one without thinking of the other. Done right, it's a relationship that works extremely well for the sponsors, the entertainers and the consumers. Of course, one of the primary reasons for using celebrities is the interest the news media take in them. In the next chapter we'll see how all of these components, woven into an effective public relations campaign, can reach out to an even greater audience.

Lou congratulating Billy Johnson, Olympic Gold Medalist, for winning the first Jeep King of the Mountain downhill competition on CBS, 1996.

Checklist

- Entertainment and celebrities should be chosen for how they complement and support your event's theme, rather than for their fame or current popularity.

- Entertainers should positively contribute to your product's image and should project credibility in the perception of your customers.

- Negotiations with celebrities and entertainers should be conducted carefully to avoid conflicts and misunderstandings later.

- Entertainment's value can be extended beyond the actual event to a much larger audience through the use of TV programming and your event's website.

Chapter 8
Public Relations

"I'd rather be called a spin doctor than a hidden persuader. Actually, I rather like the term. After all, doctors are qualified professionals, and putting the right spin on things is exactly what we do."

— Tim Bell, British advertising executive

The Cosmic Spiderweb

Talking about public relations' connection to event marketing is a little like talking about the "chicken and egg" conundrum. Which came first? Many public relations practitioners will go to great lengths to point out that, because it is a relationship-driven discipline, event marketing is actually a part of the larger public relations field. And they have a point. Creating events to support products, services or causes has long been a favorite tactic in the public relations repertoire. Events such as groundbreakings, conferences, grand openings, corporate anniversary celebrations, product launches and road shows are components in public relations programs everywhere.

Nevertheless, it is also clear that public relations plays a supporting—yet integral—role in event marketing in many ways. In my discussion of the core team, I identified public relations' primary responsibility as securing media coverage of the event. That in itself is a job that, depending on the size of the event, could occupy one person or a team of people for the duration of the event. Developing and implementing the various components of everything that comprises "media relations," in other words, is a full-time job. And it starts well before the event actually takes place. But while obtaining media coverage of the event is the primary function of public relations, the discipline can provide other valuable services as well.

Developing the story line

One of the reasons that the public relations representative sits on the core team from the beginning has to do with the discipline's role in developing and refining *messages*. Public relations experts understand that the media need stories that are compelling *and* newsworthy. A message designed for customers is not always a newsworthy message, and vice-versa. The media are especially skittish about commercial messages. Hence, the messages that attract consumers are usually not the same ones that will get media to cover the event. In fact, most reputable media outlets will avoid events they perceive as being strictly commercial. The last thing media want to do is have the public perceive them as co-opted. It destroys their credibility, thus their effectiveness as news delivery organizations.

This is not to say that public relations is supposed to "spin" the event in the sense of creating news hooks where nothing of substantial newsworthiness exists. The news angles need to be authentic, and often it takes the experienced public relations professional—someone who has worked closely with the media for a number of years—to recognize and articulate various newsworthy stories.

You may be thinking to yourself at this point, Why do I need media coverage of my event anyway? Isn't it enough to get qualified consumers there, assuming you want to position your event in the lower half of the purchase funnel? Well, of course, you are right. Reporters are not there as purchasers of your product. But because reporters and editors bring third-party credibility to the table, media coverage of your event can have a powerful effect in a number of ways.

Message validation

If you have constructed your messages honestly and effectively, media coverage of those messages can amplify and validate them to the larger consumer universe. Advertising has its place and people *do* respond to it. Nevertheless, most people are sophisticated enough to understand that advertising is self-serving, and they are at least somewhat skeptical of its claims. Of *course* an auto company is going to tell you that its vehicles are the safest, most fun to drive, most stylish, easiest handling, etc. However, by and large, these claims are subjective. If an automotive writer for a major newspaper test-drives the car and writes a story to the effect that these claims are true, they now have much more validity. In this case, the media serve as vicarious stand-ins for all the consumers that cannot attend the event. And, depending on the circulation of the newspaper or magazine or the audience of the radio or TV program, the number of people impacted can be significant.

Obviously, it's not the same as putting actual "butts in seats," but it still serves to influence consumers.

Reputation management

Positive media coverage of a successful event can reinforce your company's reputation. A robust, dynamic, positive event reflects on the company hosting it. It says to the public that your organization is innovative, vibrant and customer-oriented. Most important, depending on how interactive and "experiential" your event is, it can reflect your company's confidence in its products. It says, "We are so sure of our product's quality that we're willing for you to test it under the most rigorous of conditions." Events put a human face on your organization and products. Guests interact with real people and forge relationships that cut through the traditional corporate anonymity. Finally, the more memorable an event is, especially in terms of how it exploits the lifestyle preferences of the consumers who attend, the more customers are likely to transfer their positive feelings to the company. And effective media coverage of these event features can spread the good word on your company to a much larger audience.

Clearly, positive media coverage is very desirable. So how does the public relations team go about getting it?

Planning and preparation

As I've indicated, ideally, public relations sits at the planning table as part of the core team. In addition, the public relations team participates in pre-event site visits. During these visits, they collect the information necessary to recommend locations for media tents, plan media tours, identify venues for receptions and dinners, and even preview accommodations for editors and reporters attending the event. Throughout the planning and preparation stage, the public relations representative liaisons continually with the event team leader and program managers to ensure that issues relating to media are addressed and resolved.

Media kit and other materials

Once the public relations person or team has identified the newsworthy angles and story possibilities arising out of the event, it's time to develop the tools to tell those stories effectively. This is usually done through the development of a *media kit*—a package of materials that presents information to reporters and other media representatives in a way that showcases the newsworthy elements in a format that media types are comfortable with. Media kit contents may include:

• **Media kit folders**—with attractive and thematically appropriate covers.

• **News releases**—the basic informational vehicle for the media. In one or two pages it delivers the essential information, including the newsworthy angle, the dates and times, the major event features and attractions, and other vital information.

• **Fact sheets**—contain interesting and entertaining factoids about the event and serve as a handy resource guide for reporters. For example, fact sheets might include items on the history of the event, its attendance figures, celebrities and products.

• **Frequently asked questions**—a quick reference guide for members of the media to help them get oriented with the key data they need.

• **Product descriptions**—data and specifications sheets on products along with photos and diagrams as appropriate.

• **CD-ROMs**—containing product photos, logos, event photography, celebrities and other visually attractive materials.

In addition to the contents of the media kit, the public relations team will be responsible for developing other informational materials, such as:

• **Key messages**—the focused, primary information units for the media. These reflect the main thrust or rationale for the event, or encapsulate the five or six vital pieces of information the company wants to deliver to its audiences.

• **Media list**—containing all the media that might have an interest in the event. With the segmentation of the media over the past few years to appeal to a more diverse audience, the typical media list has grown longer and has become more diversified. But that's all good. It means you have that many more opportunities for media coverage.

"Public relations for an event is as important as the event itself."

In today's world, an event that doesn't achieve amplification beyond the event itself risks the possibility of not achieving the impact necessary to support it. Whereas public relations for event marketing used to be seen as a support function, it is now fully equivalent to the event itself in determining how successful the event will be. The explosion of media outlets has provided a greater opportunity for exposure of your event, but it has also expanded the opportunities for competitors to provide fodder for the expanded media.

• **Query letters**—to segmented media with specific story angles appropriate to the different media.

• **Media advisories**—to generate media interest and coverage. Media advisories are typically one-page bulletins containing the basic facts of the event—what, where, when, etc.

• **Media invitations**—to specific media events such as previews and receptions.

• **Media event agenda/activities guides**—for activities of interest primarily to reporters.

But the public relations function isn't confined to producing written materials. Public relations practitioners also take an active role in publicizing the event. Much of this role takes place before the event and may include the following activities:

• **Media training**—To ensure that company spokespersons feel comfortable giving interviews or news conferences that might come up as part of the event, the PR firm or representative may offer media training. This usually consists of simulating media contacts and coaching spokespersons in the use of key messages and how to respond to reporters' questions in a way that best represents the company and the event.

• **Distribution of the news releases or photo releases**— Using the media list it developed, the public relations firm or representative will distribute news and photo releases through a variety of channels including mail, email and wire services.

• **One-on-one follow-up media contact**—To encourage specific coverage, the public relations person will aggressively seek positive media coverage of and attendance at the event. This is where the public relations function really earns its money—by understanding the specific needs of the various media and tailoring the approach to meet those needs. This process puts the public relations person in touch with a broad spectrum of media, including local and national TV and radio stations (including the cable stations), lifestyle publications, syndicated programs, trade publications and consumer-oriented publications, just to name a few.

• **Production of video and audio news releases**—These are prepackaged stories on the event that stations with small staffs and limited resources often use during their news broadcasts.

• **Attendance at media events**—Media receptions and previews are a part of most large events. The public relations representative will handle the logistics for these events, often including lodging and transportation for reporters and hosting of events.

• **Other on-site activities**—including hosting and entertaining of the media, on-site newswire and photography transmission.

Once the event is over, the role of public relations continues with monitoring and post-event analysis. This includes the following:

• **Post-event media support**—working with the media to fulfill their needs after the event, such as supplying photos, follow-up interviews and leveraging other post-event opportunities. Public relations will also attempt to confirm future air dates or run dates for stories on the event (many of which can take place weeks or even months after the actual event).

• **Comprehensive media monitoring**—one of the most important functions the public relations representative performs is compiling and analyzing the media coverage of the event. This process entails capturing the coverage through audiotapes, videotapes and newspaper and magazine clips into a compilation with a report that discusses not only the quantity but also the quality of the news coverage. This is an indispensable part of the overall measurement process to determine the effectiveness of the event.

 • **Analysis/final report**—ideally, the PR firm or representative will develop a comprehensive After Action Report (AAR) summarizing the PR successes and future opportunities for improvement. The AAR should also contain an indication of the Return on Investment (ROI) provided by PR. Finally, the report should also contain recommendations for future events.

What about the difference between trade media and the general or consumer media?

If you haven't worked with the news media extensively, it's possible that you don't make a distinction between trade media and general or consumer media. Trade publications refer to magazines and other media such as newsletters and e-zines, that cover a specific industry or business. General publications, as the name suggests, have a broader audience. Neither is better than the other, although, by their nature, general publications usually have larger audiences than trade publications. The following excerpt of an interview with former *Special Events* magazine editor Liese Gardner focuses on some of the major differences between the two media.

> "It's more difficult to get press in consumer publications. First, you are competing with many, many other companies for the editor's attention, so you need a great story angle. Second, unfortunately, the media right now is [sic] fixated on any event with, by or for a celebrity or any planner who has done work with a celebrity currently in the news. So, unless there is a celebrity involved. . . Trade press is won-

derful because the magazines are targeted for a specific reader. Plus, some of these magazines are read by potential clients such as hotels, corporations, planners, etc. Although still competitive, it's a little easier to get into these types of publications, especially if you research the magazine's editorial focus and send in a story idea that directly speaks to that publication's readership."

In terms of researching the editorial focus of trade publications, the best thing to do is call the publication and ask for a current media kit. These kits include editorial calendars, information on readership and advertisers and, usually, sample issues of the publication after these are available on-line. They also include editorial information for getting in touch with the right people when you get around to pitching the magazine on your event.

The role of public relations in the overall event marketing function is comprehensive. As we will see in the next chapter, it even extends to crisis management. That's because one of the major goals of the public relations effort is to maintain a company's good reputation. It does that by understanding the dynamic relationship between an organization and *all* of its various publics, from customers to local officials, the media, vendors and suppliers—even employees and company management.

How to find a public relations firm

If you have the budget for it, hiring a competent public relations firm is the best way to ensure that your event gets publicized effectively. Following are some tips that will help in your search for a public relations firm.

- *First, it's important to recognize that not all firms that call themselves public relations firms really are public relations companies.* Unfortunately, anybody can call themselves public relations practitioners. When in doubt, ask if the firm's principals are members (better yet, Accredited Members) of the Public Relations Society of America.

- *Keep in mind that public relations firms come in all shapes and sizes.* Many public relations "firms" are actually sole proprietorships. At the other extreme are the large multinational firms with offices in most major markets. Size doesn't necessarily indicate a firm's quality, but, given the extent of activities required for a major event, including the need for on-site assistance to handle media, coordinate media events, etc., a one-person shop usually isn't practical.

- *The firms you are considering should have some experience in handling special events.* It's an unusual public relations firm that doesn't have some experience in special events, but they do exist. A firm that can demonstrate expertise in special events will have insights into some of the challenges you face in putting together an event and will be able to offer valuable counsel in this area.

- *The firm you hire should have considerable local and national media relations experience.* Since most of the PR firm's responsibilities will focus on media relations, this competency takes priority. Even though it might seem intuitive that a public relations firm would have expertise in media relations, some firms actually don't. They might specialize in community relations or employee communications or some other communications discipline that doesn't require that they get involved in media relations. Ask the firms you are considering to talk about their experience in media relations connected to special events.

• *Ask to meet the day-to-day contact at the public relations firm who will be responsible for your account.* You will likely be spending a lot of time with this person on-site at your event, and there's a lot to be said for compatibility under circumstances that are often stressful.

• *Finally, determine whether the PR firm you are interested in hiring has any expertise* in crisis management. As we will see in Chapter 10, crises are very real possibilities during events, and the more experience and skill in crisis management you can draw on, the more likely you will be to weather the crisis, should one emerge.

Checklist

- While the major responsibility of public relations is media relations—getting quality coverage of the event and managing the dynamics of that process—other PR activities are also important.

- Public relations is also involved in developing the event story line, helping validate event messages and protecting/enhancing the reputation of the company or organization hosting the event.

- Another responsibility of PR is the packaging of the event for the media—the news releases, fact sheets and other data that serve as media source material.

- PR can make an indispensable contribution in the areas of media training of event spokespersons and in the development of crisis management programs.

Chapter 9
Event Marketing and Multicultural Consumers

"Civilization is a slow process of adopting the ideas of minorities."

— Anonymous

Ideally, event marketing should be the most democratic and inclusive of marketing approaches. All of the characteristics I reviewed in Chapter 1 support this inclusiveness—the concept of wanting to connect to an audience without a mediator, the inviting and interactive nature of event marketing and, especially, the idea of event marketing's relevance to consumers—all of these attributes can easily appeal to a diverse consumer base.

However, in practice, event marketers—like their brethren in other marketing disciplines—have often fallen short when it comes to reaching out to multicultural audiences. In this chapter, we'll look at some of the challenges multiculturalism presents to the event marketer and how the tremendous opportunities in multicultural event marketing can be transformed into marketing success.

Event marketing and the multicultural consumer experience

The benefits of event marketing aren't limited to what are some-

189

times euphemistically referred to as "general" consumers. The multicultural market offers huge potential as well, as the following statistics demonstrate:

- 37 percent of the U.S. population is now multicultural, with African-Americans, Hispanics and Asians representing 28 percent of the total U.S. population, according to the 2000 Census.

- By the year 2010, 50 percent of all persons in the U.S. age 21 and under will be multicultural.

- Multicultural buying power grew by 132 percent between 1990 and 2002—from $657 billion to over $1.5 trillion (source: Selig Center/University of Georgia).

- That $1.5 trillion would be exceeded only by the GDPs of the United States, China, Japan, France and Germany.

- By 2010, multicultural buying power is estimated to increase to $2.4 trillion (source: Selig Center/ University of Georgia.)

And what does the multicultural community buy with this awesome purchasing power? Research shows that multicultural consumers show a high propensity toward premium brands such as new and luxury vehicles, communications technology and other high-end items. Even more significant, their buying preferences aren't confined to their own communities. In fact, multicultural consumers have significant influence on trends in popular culture.

- 60 percent percent of white consumers purchase hip-hop music.

- Hollywood is producing and distributing more movies that appeal to multicultural audiences (Will Smith has generated over $1 billion in box office receipts).

- "Urban" apparel now has sales in excess of $58 billion annually, representing 34 percent of the total domestic fashion industry.

In addition, multicultural consumers are spending at rates *higher* than white consumers across a growing number of categories:

- Entertainment—twice as fast as compared to white consumers (1999 New American Strategies Group Market Basket Study)

- New Vehicles—twice as fast as compared to white consumers (same source as above)

- New Homes—over two-thirds faster than white consumers (same source as above)

- Clothing—one-third faster as compared to white consumers (same source as above)

- Healthcare—three times faster as compared to white consumers

- Personal Care—two-thirds faster as compared to white consumers

You get the picture; the critical mass of multicultural consumers represents an opportunity that can't be overlooked. But it even goes beyond that. With the shift of so much wealth in the direction of multicultural markets, companies stand to actually experience an erosion of share, volume and profits if they miss the boat on multicultural marketing.

Multicultural marketing for the right reasons

Multicultural consumers have at least been on the radar of the marketing departments of many companies for several decades. In terms of event marketing, the earliest forays of corporate America into the multicultural world

Contrary to what many people might think, rodeo has a long tradition of African-American participation, boasting some of the most popular and accomplished riders.

consisted of representation at events like the N.A.A.C.P. Freedom Fund Dinner or the Black Expo. Companies would buy a table, often out of a sense of obligation—or self-preservation. In other words, these companies were buying goodwill (or insurance, depending on your point of view), forestalling criticism from the likes of Jesse Jackson and Al Sharpton and potential boycotts of their products at some unspecified time in the future.

This "affirmative action" impulse is not necessarily a bad approach, but it should not be the primary reason for focusing event marketing on multicultural markets. What is the right reason? Again, it gets back to sound business strategy. The goal of multicultural marketing should be share, volume and profits.

The other problem with the way some companies sought representation at multicultural events in the past was that they were basically anonymous, which didn't do anything for the visibility or memorability of the various brands involved. What you would typically see at a multicultural event was the "corporate ghetto," a row of indistinguishable booths along which attendees would walk with their complimentary plastic shopping bags picking up their complimentary giveaways at each of the booths. A ballpoint pen here, a keychain there. Sure, the corporate logo of each of these sponsors was affixed to each of these items, but when the attendees got home, those items went into the junk drawer in the kitchen. For all the questionable goodwill this approach might create, it did little to grow share among multicultural consumers.

Why were these efforts so feeble? Part of it has to do with a lack of confidence among marketers that they know how to reach out to multicultural consumers. Certainly there are cultural barriers to overcome—language, customs and attitudes. Partly, it was a matter of erroneous assumption—assuming, for example, that minority groups didn't have any money or didn't buy specific products. Of course, as we've seen from some of the statistics above, that kind of thinking is not only incorrect, but costly. Whatever the reasons, American companies are only slowly coming around when it comes to marketing to the multicultural community, and this includes event marketing. *Multicultural Marketing News*, an on-line newsletter, recently noted that only 10 percent of American companies were "getting it right" when it comes to multicultural marketing, while another 25 percent are "almost there." Unfortunately, the study reported that 10 percent of companies are just "checkin' it out," and a whopping 55 percent are still experiencing "trial and error." In short, corporate America is still in disarray when it comes to multicultural marketing.

It's not just about race

Keep in mind as well that *multicultural* refers not only to race and ethnicity but also to age, gender, disabilities and even sexual preference. In planning your marketing event, don't jump to conclusions about who buys what in the American household. For example, whereas the conventional wisdom might indicate that men make most of the decisions about what vehicle to buy, the fact is that 80 percent of vehicle purchasing decisions are made by women. Also, make sure your event isn't subtly excluding segments of the population—limiting access to the handicapped, for example, by not providing a barrier-free environment.

Tokenism

In the effort to be inclusive and appeal to a wider market by expanding your cultural outreach, the greatest danger lies, ironically, in marginalizing minorities within the environment of your event. This is like making sure you include an African-American or Hispanic exhibit tent at your event for no other reason than to demonstrate your "sensitivity" to these cultures. This approach has the effect of isolating multicultural consumers rather than including them. It's also condescending and, therefore, insulting. At its worst,

"Pigmentation is not the same as expertise."

A common misperception among marketers is that, if "diversity" is represented on their staffs by members of minority populations, it follows that those representatives speak for the population  segments of which they are part. This is often a fatal fallacy when it comes to appealing to multicultural audiences. Sure, minority staff members can have insights and knowledge based on their life experiences, but even within minority communities, these experiences vary greatly. Not all African-Americans, for example, are into hip hop. You need to draw on a number of resources, not least of which is primary research into multicultural communities themselves.

this attitude can result in damaged relationships with multicultural consumers, as in the infamous case of a leading car company that ran an ad in *Jet* magazine seeking to promote a vehicle to African-American consumers with the tagline: "Unlike your boyfriend, it goes to work every day." This overreaching effort is totally unnecessary.

As Steve Climons, president and creative director of Crossover Creative Group, a San Francisco-based ad agency, pointed out in an article in *DiversityInc.com*, efforts such as the example above are "patronizing and say that the company just wants my money and doesn't care to create a relationship with me."

One way that we avoided this pitfall at DaimlerChrysler was to tap deeply into customer history and values as a means of making the connection Climons refers to. When the renowned gospel group the Winans offered DaimlerChrysler the sponsorship of its 2002 Winans Family Reunion Tour, the offer was based on a long-standing relationship with the family. The union between DaimlerChrysler and the Winans began almost 50 years earlier when the family patriarch, Pop Winans, purchased a Chrysler New Yorker station wagon as his family's first vehicle. The Winans' loyalty to Chrysler continued with more Chrysler vehicle purchases over the years.

Beyond the typical benefits of such a sponsorship—visibility, media coverage, promotional opportunities—DaimlerChrysler's connection to the Winans tour appealed to a specific demographic group—African-Americans—with specific lifestyle preferences—an interest in gospel music—without the appearance of multicultural opportunism on DaimlerChrysler's part. Why? Because the rationale for the sponsorship had a long continuity of mutual respect.

The lesson here is that it's sometimes possible to overdo it in the effort to appeal to multicultural audiences. So, what is necessary? Often it's more a matter of nuance. At the least it means exposing yourself to other cultures and understanding their specific needs and aspirations. There are several ways to begin this process.

• *Familiarize yourself with the multicultural media*—As is the case with all forms of media today, the outlets are expanding. There are magazines, TV and radio shows (and sometimes entire stations) and Internet websites devoted to multicultural audiences. These can be excellent sources of information on what issues and concerns affect minority audiences.

• *Keep up with the research*—The exploding multicultural market is spawning new research into the buying habits of minority groups on almost a continual basis. Staying current with these research sources can help you to identify trends in multicultural marketing that you can use in your events.

• *Forge partnerships* with institutions and organizations important to multicultural consumers. For many ethnic and minority groups, these groups are anchors of and gateways into the community. Partnering with them is one way to reach deeper into the community.

The following example shows how one company effectively enhanced its bond with its multicultural consumer base by tapping into the unique and rich historical phenomenon of the black experience in America. Sterling Greene, who was instrumental in the success of this event, is my source for this case study.

Case Study: Western Union hits a home run at Black Expo

At the 1997 Black Expo in Atlanta, the title sponsor was Chrysler, but the sponsor that received the most notice did so with an ingenious exhibit that tapped into black American culture within the broader context of America's century-old love affair with the National Pastime.

As a sponsoring partner in Black Expo, Western Union had a significant rationale for its appearance. The company has been in the money transfer business since 1871, just two years, by the way, after the first professional baseball team—the Cincinnati Red Stockings—took the field for the first time. Western Union's domestic money transfer business is heavily populated by minorities—as much as 80 percent of the business in some markets.

Tapping into this history, Western Union decided to build an exhibit that would dominate this event. The impetus for the exhibit was the fact that 1997 was the 50th anniversary of Jackie Robinson's breaking into the Major Leagues with the Brooklyn Dodgers. Digging a little deeper into this fact, the developers of the Western Union event researched the history of Negro Leagues baseball in the United States, learning that there existed, in fact, a museum of the leagues in Kansas City. As a result of this research, the company decided to construct a 2,000-square-foot, floor-to-ceiling replica of a baseball stadium. The exhibit contained photos and other displays, and even some interactive elements. For example, in one area, kids could throw the ball to a representation of Josh Gibson, the legendary Negro Leagues catcher, and could win prizes.

The exhibit was such a hit that the local TV and radio stations did their remote news broadcasts from the exhibit, and a survey of people leaving the event revealed that most attendees thought Western Union was the title sponsor of Black Expo that year.

This is just one example of how the minority experience in American culture can be celebrated with dignity and taste while still meeting sound business objectives. The next case study looks at how the Sara Lee company met a somewhat different challenge in the Hispanic market.

Case Study: Sara Lee says, "Let's eat!"

Challenge

- Create awareness and brand equity of select Sara Lee products (Sara Lee, Jimmy Dean, Hillshire Farm, Ball Park, Mazola).

- Develop a platform for Sara Lee brands to be present in the Hispanic market.

- Form a strong association between Sara Lee and the following qualifiers:

  —Quality ingredients

  —Convenience

  —Saving time

  —The brand that understands your life

The solution

Lápiz, Relay Event Marketing, and Tapestry Partners, experts in Hispanic marketing, devised and executed the *A Comer* Sampling Program on behalf of Sara Lee to introduce select brands to Hispanic consumers via an engaging grass roots effort. *A Comer* (in English it means "let's eat") was a celebration of food that offers Hispanic mothers who are entrusted with preparing meals for their families a chance to experience delicious Sara Lee products.

Program overview

The cornerstone of the program was a grass-roots tour that included cooking demonstrations, sampling of products, and contests and games. This grass-roots effort was supported by:

- A consumer sweepstakes promotion
- In-store point-of-sale displays
- A radio advertising campaign
- A PR campaign

Lou Bitonti

Target audience

Spanish-dominant mothers, age 25-49, who

- Take pride in their roles as gatekeeper
- Are the primary meal preparers and providers for their families
- Consider well-being of their families as a top priority
- Provide both physical and emotional nourishment

Event marketing component: The *A Comer* Mobile Kitchen Tour

A state-of-the-art kitchen on wheels participated in festivals, events and key Hispanic retail venues. Each appearance was highlighted by cooking demonstrations performed by a professional chef, sampling of prepared foods, music, games and contests.

The chef spokesperson was Daniel Olivella, whose name is synonymous with the best Spanish food. He was supported by Sara Lee Ambassadors, a fully trained and bilingual staff.

Results

Consumers reacted favorably to the A Comer Sampling Program, especially many who were unfamiliar with Sara Lee products and responded enthusiastically once they tasted them. The most popular recipes were the Sara Lee Smoked Turkey Quesadilla, the Jimmy Dean Torta, the Polka Kielbasa and shrimp skewers in a mustard sauce. Most of the consumers were glad to learn how easy these recipes were to prepare at home.

Other benefits of the event

- The *A Comer* multi-brand promotion successfully generated awareness of participating brands among Hispanic consumers.

- There were strong indications the promotion positively impacted sales.

   (Based on retail store manager questionnaires and on-site consumer surveys.)

Chapter Checklist

Checklist

- Multicultural consumers represent a large and growing market that companies can't ignore if they want to hold on to share, volume and profits.

- Historically, companies have had an "affirmative action" event marketing approach to multicultural consumers that functioned more as an insurance policy against protest than an active marketing campaign.

- Membership in a minority group does not equate to expertise in consumer motivations and preferences.

- It's possible to try too hard in efforts to appeal to multicultural consumers, with the unintended consequences of tokenism and alienation.

- Effective event marketing to multicultural audiences recognizes and taps into common values and heritage.

Chapter 10

What About When Things Go Wrong?

"Everything in the universe is subject to change and everything
is right on schedule."

— A corporate mystic

The Cosmic Spiderweb

No matter how seamless an event appears to an outsider, or even to a participant, every event has its crisis moments. It's the nature of the activity. Events are complex and complicated. They often take place in environments where some external forces can't be controlled. Weather, for example, can be anticipated, but not controlled. The same is true for other natural phenomena such as (depending on the area of the country you're in) earthquakes, fires and flooding.

More importantly, events involve people, sometimes a great number of people. And human nature—and behavior—is often unpredictable. Individual behavior is frequently magnified by the crowd mentality. Just think of the many tragic cases of panic erupting in crowded stadiums, entertainment arenas and nightclubs over the past few years. In most of these cases, the panic and the resulting injuries and deaths were exacerbated by poor or nonexistent planning. My purpose here is not to discourage you from holding an event, but to point out that crises are inevitable and that preparation can minimize their impact. The greatest sin is to assume that it won't happen to you.

If the crisis is contained early enough, often people are unaware that it ever happened. But the more magnitude a crisis assumes, the more noticeable it becomes and the more potential it has for giving your event the *wrong* kind of memorability.

Rule #1

Crises are going to occur. That's why the first rule of crisis management is to acknowledge that you cannot prevent every crisis from happening. As I've already pointed out, too many things are out of the control of the event manager. The best you can do is to anticipate crises and prepare for them. That way, their impact can be minimized. The biggest mistake an event manager can make—you could call it the Titanic Syndrome—is to assume his or her event is so airtight that nothing can go wrong. That leads us to Rule #2.

Rule #2

While you can't prevent all crises from occurring, you can take steps to manage them effectively, minimize their impacts and preserve—and even enhance—your company's reputation in the process.

Preventive measures

One of the first things you need to do as you plan an event is protect yourself and your organization from those disasters—or mere inconveniences —that you can anticipate. One of the very important functions of your legal representative is to play devil's advocate, in a sense. He or she will need to analyze your vulnerabilities from a legal standpoint and recommend the necessary actions. These necessary actions may include the following:

• **Incorporation.** As a first step, legal counsel will often recommend that the event be set up as a separate corporation to protect the event managers, attendees, media and other entities from liability. In the case of charitable events, this corporation can be set up as a tax-exempt foundation through 501 (c) (3) status.

• **Obtaining insurance coverage.** A number of insurance companies specialize in insuring events. They may provide coverage for weather, fires, accidents and other potentially damaging occurrences. You can even get insurance for hole-in-one contests at golf events and for rock-wall climbing. Insurance companies also provide personal injury policies and liability insurance. Since each event is unique, it is important to speak to a representative of one of these companies to get a clear picture of the exact coverages required for any given event. A reputable insurance agency will typically review the site and make recommendations for coverage based on an analysis of the risks. Most will recommend umbrella policies as well as specific coverages, depending on the nature of the event.

• **Drafting waivers.** Typically, event managers will require that attendees fill out and sign waivers to protect against lawsuits. For example, if an attendee wants to try out a treadmill at a health and fitness show, he or she would most likely have to sign a waiver stating that the event's hosts, the manufacturer and other parties are not responsible should the attendee be injured or suffer an adverse reaction such as a heart attack or stroke. Such waivers need to be worded appropriately and with an awareness of applicable laws and ordinances. That kind of work is best left to legal minds.

• **Negotiating contracts and agreements.** What happens if the venue you've chosen for your event is damaged by a storm? What happens if the labor union that represents the workers who will unload your trucks goes on strike? If your celebrity decides he or she has a better offer elsewhere and decides to take it instead of doing your event, what recourse do you have? These are just some examples of issues that your legal counsel will work out in advance through negotiations.

EVENT INSURANCE QUOTESMITH

There are three things you need to know about event insurance: One, most venues require it. Two, you need to protect your company's assets should anyone get hurt, and peace of mind runs a distant third. Use this worksheet compiled for *Event Marketer* by the super-serious agents at Woburn, MA-based ASU International (ASUI.com), as a quick guide to the five types of major event insurance.

Protect Your Brand, Your Customers—And Yourself.

TYPE 1 -- SPECIAL EVENT LIABILITY COVERAGE

Why you need it:

- Whether you are running a small sampling program or a major event, you can be exposed to some problematic legal liabilities.

- Brands/sponsors may require their agencies indemnify them for any and all liability related to the event or marketing campaign.

- Annual general liability policies may not be suitable to properly respond to single-event risks. Potential coverage gaps may exist.

- A special-event liability policy insuring a single event will avoid dilution of an annual policy's limits of insurance and provide specific coverage for the event.

What it covers:

- The policy covers third-party bodily injury or property damage that arises out of the special event.

- The policy allows you to extend "Additional Insured" status to a venue owner or sponsor. (Athletic activities are usually excluded, but such coverage can be added to the policy.)

TYPE 2 -- EVENT CANCELLATION COVERAGE

Why you need it:

- In many cases, event organizers and sponsors have a significant financial exposure if an event has to be cancelled, postponed or relocated.

  Event marketers face the loss of production costs and revenue-generating opportunities if the event does not go on as planned.

What it covers:

- This policy responds to the financial loss sustained by an event sponsor or organizer as a result of cancellation, postponement or abandonment of an event for reasons beyond their control.

- Policies can include coverage for weather, terrorism, satellite or signal failure, nonappearance of performers and key personnel.

- Loss of ticket sales, advertising revenue, event production costs and sponsorship monies can be protected under the policy.

TYPE 3 -- WEATHER INSURANCE

Why you need it:

- Adverse weather can reduce event attendance and negatively impact the potential revenue from the event. With this policy, even though the event may not be cancelled, organizers can still have insurance protection for lost revenue as well as expenses necessary to stage the event.

What it covers:

- Event weather is most often provided as a risk-management tool to single-day or weekend event programs.

- Adverse weather is insured against during a specified time period.

- It is designed to offset revenue lost or expenses incurred due to reduced attendance at the insured event.

- Reduction in ticket sales and various other insurable interests including concessions, food and parking are also covered.

TYPE 4 -- NON-OWNED AND HIRED AUTOMOBILE COVERAGE

Why you need it:

- Event marketers, promoters and/or their agencies have legal liability exposures relating to the use of any non-owned vehicles in conjunction with event marketing activities.

What it covers:

- The holder of the policy receives automobile liability coverage for bodily injury to others and their damaged property while using a non-owned or hired vehicle in the course of planning or executing event marketing programs.

- Optional coverage for damage to the actual non-owned or rented vehicle can be added to the coverage for an additional charge.

TYPE 5 -- TRIP ACCIDENT COVERAGE

Why you need it:

- Participants in an event or winners of promotional trips may become ill or get injured in conjunction with these activities. Injured parties could take legal action against the event marketer, the agency or the sponsor.

What it covers:

- Accidental death and dismemberment coverage for participants or winners of trip prizes, including special events.

- The policy pays a fixed benefit level to the injured person without regard to legal liability.

- This guaranteed 24-hour, worldwide benefit can help diminish the chance of an incident resulting in a legal action.

INFORMATION REQUIRED BY INSURERS FOR POLICY ESTIMATES

- Venue/location

- Date(s) of the event

- Attendance per day

- Total revenue projected

- List of key talent associated with the event

- Names and addresses of any trip winners

- Total expenses

- Cost to rent non-owned automobiles

- Additional Insured list—your client and/or venue

- Security plan

- Details on sports or athletic events

- Details about the serving or sale of liquor

Contingency plans

A crisis need not totally ruin an event. By putting contingency plans in place where possible, the event can go forward with a minimum of disruption. For example, depending on availability, you may be able to secure an alternative location should your original site become unavailable for any reason. Obviously, this will work more easily for smaller events, but even in large open areas, you might query the local residents and commercial land owners to determine how willing they might be to reserve property as a backup location.

As I mentioned earlier, part of the site selection and review process involves meeting with local police, fire and emergency medical departments to determine their capacity to assist with any crisis that may develop. Should an attendee become seriously injured or ill and need to be evacuated quickly, what will be the procedure? Is a helicopter available? What kinds of injuries is the local medical facility capable of handling? Is the local police force trained in crowd control procedures? What is the response time for the fire department and what kinds of fires are they capable of containing? All of these and more issues should be ironed out with the local authorities well before the event takes place.

What we have been talking about so far are precautions. You need to take them wherever possible. But you also need to prepare for the worst.

Crisis management

The process of planning for and managing a crisis is called *crisis management*. Many people think of crisis management as reactive, something put into effect to control damage. That's part of what crisis management is, but the discipline is more than reactive. In fact, true crisis management starts well

"Live by Murphy's Law."

Murphy's Law states that if anything can go wrong, it will. The law has a number of corollaries that are also worth reviewing by anyone in the event marketing field ("Nothing is as easy as it looks" and "Everything takes longer than you think" are two of the more appropriate corollaries for event marketers, for example.) I never really knew what Murphy's Law was all about until I got into event marketing. Things will go wrong; the world, people and events are not perfect, so be prepared.

before any crises occur, and sometimes crises are averted because of effective crisis management.

People often equate "crisis" with "emergency." This, unfortunately, leads them to think of crises as uncontrollable events, catastrophes that arise independent of any causality. This leads, in turn, to a mindset that says, "Even if something goes wrong, we can't be held responsible. It was an accident. There's nothing we can do about it." The problem with this line of reasoning is that your various audiences aren't likely to see it that way. And they're right. In truth, the "emergency" is only the most visible phase of the crisis continuum. Damage from a crisis isn't confined to those immediately affected. An unmanaged crisis can overwhelm the entire organization, all the way back to the boardroom of the headquarters building hundreds or thousands of miles away.

In his book *The Crisis Counselor: A Step-by-Step Guide to Managing a Business Crisis,* Jeffrey R. Caponigro talks about the true crisis management mindset as a series of seven important steps:

1. Identify and assess vulnerabilities in the organization.

For purposes of event marketing, this can be rendered as identify and assess vulnerabilities *throughout the event marketing process.* This means taking a systematic look at what can go wrong, not only based on past history but also being imaginative enough to anticipate crises that have never happened before. This "vulnerabilities audit" encourages event managers to become aware of the potential for a crisis, which is the first step in being able to manage one effectively. Caponigro recommends ranking potential crises according to their "likelihood of occurrence" and their potential for "damage to the business." The rankings can then be combined to determine a crisis priority list.

2. Prevent the vulnerabilities from erupting into crises.

Once you've identified potential crises, you need to take the necessary preventive steps to avoid them. If, for example, one of your vulnerabilities is the poten-

214

Lou with Lee Iacocca, a man who knew a thing or two about how to handle a crisis, at the Jeep King of the Mountain ski event.

tial collapse of a tent, you need to make sure that the support structures are reinforced and that there is an evacuation plan and plenty of highly visible exits.

3. Plan for a potential crisis. You prevent where you can, but you still plan for the worst. As I mentioned earlier, crises are inevitable. It's how you handle them that counts. Planning for a crisis means putting together a written document that lays out the steps necessary for managing the crisis. This includes emergency steps to be taken, people to be notified (broken out by audiences such as emergency responders, employees and their families, attendees, company management and other stakeholders), names and contact numbers for spokespersons, and basic key messages. The plan should also include fact sheets, backgrounders and other information on the event to supplement reporters' stories as well as reporting forms to complete for documentation of contacts with the media and others.

4. Identify when a crisis has occurred and determine actions to be taken. Timing is critically important during a crisis. Action needs to be taken quickly and decisively, not only to minimize the actual impact of the crisis but also to demonstrate to key audiences that you know how to take charge during these times.

5. Communicate most effectively during a crisis. By their nature, crises attract attention. They also provoke questions. Depending on the severity of the crisis, the news media may even take an interest. Not communicating with your key audiences during a crisis is not an option. Lack of communication encourages the spread of rumors, gives the impression that you are hiding something or that you don't know how to manage the situation, and can be downright dangerous if the information you fail to report could have saved lives and protected property. Most of the time, an organization's reluctance to communicate during a crisis stems from liability issues or the fear that the media will distort what you have said. What people often fail to realize is that these fears can be allayed by effective, ongoing communications. Once again, from *The Crisis Counselor*, here are Caponigro's general tips for communicating during a crisis:

• *Identify all the various publics who may be affected by—or expect to be informed about—the crisis.* This is an important step. The discipline of identifying all your publics helps ensure that you don't leave an important audience out. It also helps you to prioritize your notification.

• *Prove that you have identified the problem and are doing something about it.* People will forgive accidents, even when human error is involved. What they won't tolerate during a crisis is inaction. Even if you can only say you are investigating the situation and implementing your crisis management plan, it's better than demonstrating paralysis in the face of a crisis.

• *Communicate a small number of core messages to the appropriate publics.* It's usually impossible to cover every aspect of crisis while it's in progress. By repeating core messages ("Our crisis management team is in place and is evaluating the situation"), you convey confidence and control.

• *Communicate only what can be confirmed with absolute certainty.* The tendency during a crisis is to pounce on any good news, but resist this temptation. If your good news turns out to be not so good, you've lost a measure of credibility—nothing's more important than credibility during a crisis.

• *Don't lie about anything.* Speaking of credibility, it should go without saying that lying is fatal to it. And I'm not talking about the big lies. Usually, it's the little white lies that come back to haunt you. These occur most often when spokespersons are trying to minimize the crisis. Sometimes it's as innocent as wishful thinking. But you should avoid lying at all costs.

• *Don't comment on hypothetical situations.* It's easy to fall into the "what if" trap. That's why asking hypothetical questions is one of the news media's favorite techniques. But your spokesperson is not a fortune teller. Stick to what is known; refrain from commenting on hypotheticals.

• *Convey a strong sense that you'll be accessible and communicative.* If you are the spokesperson for a marketing event that experiences a crisis, remember to remain visible. Communicate on a regular basis, even if there isn't much to report (usually there will be at least one tidbit of new information to offer). Your publics need to be reassured that you're not going to disappear in the middle of a crisis.

• *Be decisive.* In a crisis, you need to project confidence and a willingness to take action. Hesitancy and vacillation will be perceived as your being at the mercy of the crisis.

• *Keep your cool.* Any panic or anger on your part will instantly be transmitted to your audiences. Project confidence and calmness.

• *Don't say "no comment" to the news media or anyone else.* To your publics, who are hanging on your every announcement about the status of the crisis, "no comment" means "we've got something to hide." Plain and simple. Never say "no comment" to the media or any other public.

• *Communicate all the bad news at one time.* This may seem like hard advice to take. Your thought about your audiences might be, "How much can they take at one time?" But it's much better to get it all out in the open, rather than letting the bad news accumulate slowly over time, which starts to give the crisis an atmosphere of impending doom as your publics wait for the next in what might seem like an endless series of shoes to drop.

• *Include ways to obtain feedback and input from your publics.* Your various publics are likely to feel helpless during a crisis. They need opportunities to express their thoughts and ideas. This two-way communication also helps you gauge how effective your communications have been.

• *Document for the record.* Good records of conversations, calls, media contacts and other inquiries and responses will not only serve as a "transcript" of the crisis (helpful to lawyers and public relations people) but will also help you to determine what could be done differently or better if a similar situation occurs in the future.

• *Monitor and evaluate the situation.* Make sure your messages are reaching the correct audiences and that they are able to make use of the information you provide. Determine how your messages are being received and clarify where necessary. Monitoring and evaluating also demonstrates that you are staying on top of events.

• *Don't stop communicating.* In a communications vacuum, rumor, misinformation and outright lies and distortion will often swoop in. During a crisis, you need to maintain as much control of the communications agenda as possible so that accurate, timely information is disseminated. This means ongoing communications. And keep in mind that the tendency sometimes is to focus on the news media as the only audience. In reality, each of your audiences—

customers, employees, management, local officials, vendors and suppliers—should be kept informed.

6. Monitor and evaluate the crisis and make adjustments along the way. Although they can be traumatic, crises are opportunities to learn. If you plan to have a recurring event, evaluating the management of any crises you may encounter will enable you to determine how successfully you managed them and how you might do better in the future. Did you neglect a key audience? Put them on the list. Did you have difficulty developing clear, effective key messages? Use the feedback from your audiences to learn how to communicate better in the future. How was the media coverage of your crisis? Could it have been better? How could you have secured more accurate, balanced coverage? Did you respond quickly enough? If not, how could you have streamlined the process? If you're not sure about how well you handled the crisis, why not ask some of your key audiences? Mail a questionnaire to attendees. Do a phone survey of suppliers and vendors. Consult with local emergencies services to determine how your performance could have been better. Most people will appreciate that you have their interests at heart and will cooperate.

7. Insulate your business through activities intended to enhance your organization's reputation and credibility. When things do go wrong, the amount of goodwill you have built up with your various publics will go a long way toward protecting your company's reputation. This is why establishing and maintaining close relationships with the local communities where you intend to hold events is so important. As Caponigro points out: "When a business isn't properly insulated, it almost always receives immediate criticism and little support in times of crisis. A business without the proper insulation finds it publics jumping to a 'guilty' verdict well before it can do much about it. The key to effectively managing a crisis is to be in full control and confident, and that can occur only with the support and teamwork of the people important to the success of your business."

As these tips make clear, one of your most effective weapons in the case of a crisis is effective communications. In the next chapter, we'll look at how one communications vehicle—the Internet and the electronic communications opportunities it provides—have begun to transform event marketing's relationships with stakeholders.

Checklist

- While much about an event can be controlled, so many variables are involved that not everything about an event is predictable. The two constants are 1) not all crises can be anticipated and prevented, and 2) their impact can be minimized and they can be managed effectively. Preventive measures should be taken, including:

  –Incorporation, if applicable
  –Obtaining insurance coverage
  –Drafting the appropriate waivers
  –Correctly negotiating contracts and agreements

- Contingency plans should be designed to address emergencies.

- A crisis management plan should be developed that analyzes vulnerabilities and systematizes the crisis communications process.

Chapter 11
How Technology Has Transformed Event Marketing

"One thing is clear: We don't have the option of turning away from the future. No one gets to vote on whether technology is going to change our lives."

— Bill Gates, U.S. software entrepreneur

The Cosmic Spiderweb

Large-scale marketing events have come a long way in the past two decades both in terms of their goals and achievements, and their acceptance by marketing executives. Some events today rival Las Vegas productions in their content and the various opportunities for experiencing new and exciting things. As I've already pointed out, one of the major innovations in events has been the interactive element, which allows a fuller sense of participation to attendees than ever. No longer do your customers have to be passive consumers of messages *about* your products. They can now interact *with* your products in imaginatively constructed environments that appeal to their lifestyle preferences.

Technology's impact on event marketing covers a wide range of applications, enhancing and even shaping the events themselves. There are, however, two specific areas that are at the forefront of new technology adoption and integration. One of these areas, program performance measurement, we'll touch on in this chapter and look at in closer detail in the next chapter. The other area, consumer interaction, grows so quickly that by the time you read this chapter, much of what we discuss here will be, if not obsolete, then certainly "upgraded." That means that the best advice anyone can give you on technology as it relates to event marketing is to keep on top of it.

In terms of consumer interaction, some recent technologies that have changed the way event marketers entice, entertain and educate consumers include the following:

Datastorm and mobile satellites

This technology allows for Internet connectivity in remote locations. Typical uses include connections to a microsite created especially for the event on-line celebrity/peer chats, videoconferencing, on-line gaming and email.

Text messaging

Text messaging allows for personal, two-way communication during and after large-scale events such as concerts, festivals and professional sports contests. Typical uses of this technology include trivia and poll questions, song requests, contest giveaways, appointment and schedule reminders, and general information distribution.

Wireless technology

Wireless applications such as Bluetooth technology make events much less cluttered and more flexible as computers, kiosks and other equipment become untethered. Wireless also creates more interactive opportunities such as the use of "human kiosks" carrying laptops, tablet PCs, PDAs and advanced cell phones. This makes technology more approachable and reinforces brand messages in a more personal way.

Another popular wireless application is the opportunity to take pictures with camera phones that can immediately be sent to a server that places the pictures on a plasma screen on the event site. At Camp Jeep, we're even experimenting with giving attendees a Nikon handheld video camera to test drive, so they can film their whole event.

LED (Jumbotron and other outdoor screens)

Jumbotron has almost become the generic term for large, relatively high-definition screens that allow large crowds to view activities as one. (Jumbotron is actually a Sony trademark.) Advances and cost reductions in screens that can be clearly viewed outdoors have made TV screens carrying branded content, live events or actual real time event footage more prevalent.

CD and DVD technology

New data and video technology has become an integral part of event pre-selling, summary and recap. CDs can be used as invitations to events, and can include photos and data from previous events as well as information on event schedules, locations and enrollment.

For the 10th anniversary of Camp Jeep, we put together a DVD portraying a sample of the previous 10 years of activity as an invitation to the event. Compared to a conventional "paper" invitation, the CD or DVD brings the event to life with action, color, sound—in short, the total emotional atmosphere of the event.

Kiosks

Strategically located throughout an event's landscape, interactive kiosks, complete with computer keyboards, allow event marketers to capture data and provide opportunities for dispensing information to attendees on the host's products and services.

Games

I've discussed how events are moving into the area of virtual reality as well as real-life experiences themselves. But the growth of game technology has also created opportunities to magnify and extend the life of events by replicating them in game form. We are currently working with game manufactures to simulate in game form events such as the Jeep King of the Mountain ski events, building on the success and popularity of the event.

Tracking

The technology exists to follow attendees throughout an event to determine traffic flows, gauge the popularity of specific event attractions and to understand other dynamics that can help improve events. This can be done with chips embedded into the attendees' name badges or lanyards. We've also experimented at Camp Jeep with handheld GPS devices for attendees who want to keep track of friends and family members.

E-mail and the Internet

Probably no technological development has had more impact on event marketing than the Internet. Just as Internet technology has revolutionized every other facet of business, it has also created new opportunities for event marketing. For example, it's now possible to register for events through event websites. Event managers can track feedback from attendees through email. They can track interest in their products through the number of hits on their websites. And they can use their websites to generate interest in the events by showcasing the activities of previous events using technology such as streaming video, digital photography and other interactive features.

I've already mentioned on-line registration. Technology is available today to fully automate this process. A local Intranet can even be set up for on-

228

site registration. With this technology one can refer to a database of preregistered or invited attendees to speed up the check-in process. Those who haven't preregistered can then be added to the system on-site. From this completed database, you can determine the percentage of preregistered or invited consumers who attended the event versus those who were neither preregistered nor invited.

Chat rooms can also be created for event attendees and enthusiasts. This works especially well with events like Camp Jeep, whose attendees, we have learned through our research, enjoy a sense of community. They like gatherings, actual or virtual.

The following FAQ offers some guidelines for making effective event marketing use of websites and the Internet for event marketing.

Q. When designing an event website, what should be included?

A. Up front, the website should be designed to serve as a method of attracting people to the event (before), generating awareness of the activities and excitement at the event (during), and providing a way of capturing/documenting the event to recap for those who were unable to attend and/or remind those who attended (after). If designed properly, the event website can generate additional traffic to the event, make those who attend better prepared for and satisfied with their participation, and act as a way to make the event live on for those who experience it through the interactive medium post-completion. An event website can additionally be used to capture important data from attendees. The site should also build goodwill with people who don't attend and have no intention of ever attending.

Q. What are some design tips for an event marketing manager about how an event website should look?

A. One of the most crucial elements of the website design is to fully

"Embrace technology, but don't let it consume you."

"Techies" used to play a supporting role in event marketing, and they still do. But they have since become integral to the success of events. It's as though the equipment manager has been elevated to the tactician. That's fine. Make use of the techie's talents, but if technology is not your area of expertise, don't get involved in its minutiae. Leave it to the experts.

understand from start to finish how the event is promoted, coordinated and executed. In order to fully synchronize the on-line presence (website) with the off-line work, the website design team needs to tightly interact with the group of individuals handling the other elements of the event. The ongoing participation by the website designer in the planning meetings from the initial planning stages through post-event activities enables the designer to access information critical to the site design, maintain consistent design look and feel between the off-line elements (invitations, post cards, etc.) with the actual site design, and really leverage the efficiencies of being part of the planning team.

Q. How can an event website be used before the event, during the event and after the event?

A. Before: An event website can serve as an interactive awareness tool for individuals who have never experienced the event and desire more information before actually attending. Typically there is an element of event websites that captures photography, vide, and sometimes things similar to journal entries from former event participants. This information allows the designer to paint a fairly complete picture of an event for someone who may not know what, for example, Camp Jeep or a Jeep Jamboree is. (Note: Keep in mind that photo- and graphics-intensive pages should have links and that they require longer download times, especially on dial-up connections.)

During: Event websites can also serve a purpose *during* an event (or during a series of events). For example, event sites may contain a photo gallery that could be refreshed with photographs from the previous night's activities (for multi-day events) so that people would not only be driven on-line after the event, but also those who were attending on the previous day could see the excitement from the night before. In the case of the North American International Auto Show, for example, coordinated efforts were made to broadcast the event live on the Web to give those who could not attend a view inside without actually being present.

After: Event websites also serve the purpose of making the event live on after the event is over. One way this can be achieved for event site executions is through eShots. eShots is a service comprising a team of individuals who attend events with special equipment designed to take photographs of people participating in event activities and then drives them on-line to view and share the photograph after the event is over. It is a great way to drive post-event traffic to the Web and allows people to engage after the fun. (Keep in mind, however, that this is not an effective way to generate measurement or research. Attendees/respondents should be driven to the website to download a photo, not to complete a questionnaire.)

Q. What are the opportunities for using audio and video on event websites?

A. Audio and video are both great ways to add dimension by making the event website more interactive and experiential. In the case of Camp Jeep, for example, Organic, the firm that designed the event website, has typically included audio and video of the previous year's activities to give site visitors a chance to see off-road driving challenges, event entertainment such as musicians, and more. Audio and video are critical to the on-line presence as they make the site more engaging by appealing to some of the senses that would typically only be touched by actually experiencing the event in person. Again, use discretion when loading video clips as they take a long time to download. And never have a looping song that starts when the page is loaded. It's distracting, annoying and counterproductive to the objective of informing and entertaining a prospect.

Q. What other interactive opportunities does an event website offer?

A. First, the site can increase awareness. Through the use of on-line media (banners), websites can serve as a unique way of promoting an event in a targeted fashion.

Web sites can also serve in many ways to enhance the activity at events and improve the experience of the participant. Again, in the case of Camp Jeep, Organic coordinated efforts with BBDO, Jeep's advertising partners, to not only engage individuals for on-line registrations but also to enable on-line activity scheduling to give participants a way to better plan their time while at the event. This was a unique opportunity to help event participants better plan and organize their time on-line before attending the event.

Q. What are mistakes to avoid when building an event website?

A. Websites should typically be very consistent—both in terms of look and feel as well as information—with corresponding off-line elements. As much as possible, the website design team should focus on not only reiterating the critical information communicated in print but the Web should extend the story so that people can go deeper and learn more. If the website is inconsistent with the off-line communications or the level of information is inadequate, it may cause confusion or disinterest in the mind of potential participants.

In addition, the site should provide links to all of the most critical elements as cleanly and obviously as possible. For example, if the goal of the website during the awareness stage is to enable registrations, the website shouldn't make it difficult to find a link to a "Register Online" button. That may seem obvious, but you would be surprised how often some of the most obvious things are buried due to poor planning.

Q. How can you direct traffic to your website?

A. The most important way to drive traffic to the site is through the use of URLs (website addresses) placed very obviously in all off-line media elements such as post cards, television ads, radio spots, print publications, billboards, etc. The event's website address should also be included in all materials distributed to the media (media kits, news releases, media advisories, fact sheets, etc.)

Another method of driving traffic to the website is through the use of on-line media (banner ads). On-line media offers a unique opportunity to target individuals by placing or promoting them on sites that meet certain event demographic criteria. For example, with Jeep's "Chasing Papi" program, the on-line media placements targeted the Hispanic population (Yahoo! en Español) as well as people in certain cities (Yahoo! en Español's Miami content). This provided a unique opportunity to speak in very one-on-one fashion.

Q. How often should you change your event website?

A. The website should be updated at least as frequently as the critical information changes off-line. Obviously, all dates, schedules, "sold out" status, and pertinent information should be consistent off-line and on-line. There is an unofficial, yet general, perception that websites always contain the most current information, so the on-line presence should reflect that. In addition, if there is an opportunity to make the site more immersive by updating content more frequently than the offline communications, that should be taken into consideration. It should also be noted when the site was last updated, perhaps at the bottom. Visitors to event sites, especially, are interested in knowing exactly how current the information on the site is.

Q. What are some trends for the future in event website design and operation?

A. Future website will typically become even more interactive than they are today. As the technology improves, website can become an even more engaging way of participating without attending. There is no substitute for actually being at the event, but the Web does allow people to experience many of the event's elements in the comfort of their homes and at their own convenience. On-line media (banners) and other viral marketing tactics also will continue to develop to better target individuals to make them aware of events in which they may be interested. In the future, the website may also play a role during the event. Using new WiMax technology, attendees will be able to view what is happening right now, in real time, on their PDAs, for all the various event exhibits and activities. They can see if the exhibits have specific demonstration times or programs they don't want to miss. This helps them plan their time and enjoy a richer event experience.

Obviously, attracting people to your event's website is a critical factor in making effective use of the technology. In addition to some of the ideas offered in the FAQ above, following are some ideas for driving qualified traffic to your website, from Vince Emery, writing for *Event Marketing* magazine's on-line version.

Nine ways to drive traffic–and one to avoid

1. Get prominent listings on search engines and in Web directories. The key word here is *prominent.* When Alta Vista returns 70,000 listings to someone searching for your type of product, you don't want to be buried on the bottom. You want to be in the first page of results. For most websites, search engines and directories are the most important sources of qualified visitors. They account for 70 percent or more of the visitors to many sites. [Of course, people are not usually taking a blind stab when they are looking for an event, as is often the case with other Internet "surfers." Hence, the majority of event searches would fall into the other 30 percent.]

2. Rent or collect "opt in" email addresses and email invitations to your prospects. "Opt-in" lists consist of people who have *asked* to receive email about a specific subject. One country music site rented three separate email lists of country music fans, combined them, and emailed an announcement about a country music contest. Within eight hours, 11.6 percent of recipients visited the site. A week later, 30 percent had visited. Email lists like these are one of the best ways to build traffic quickly.

3. Beg, swap or buy links to your site from other sites your prospects visit. Associations, educational sites and other companies are likely candidates for links. What other websites do your prospects visit? See if you can get a text link from those sites to yours. Over time, they could send you a steady stream of highly qualified visitors. Sometimes you can get a link from another site just by asking. Try that approach first. Most of the time, however, you'll scratch their backs and they'll scratch yours as each of you adds links to the other. If the other site's visitors are valuable enough to you, you might even offer to pay for a link.

4. Promote your site URL off-line everywhere you can. You've seen other people's URLs (website addresses) on buses, billboards, T-shirts and TV commercials. You can do the same with yours. Put it on your letterhead, business cards and checks—anyplace you print a phone number. Make sure all your employees include your Web address in their email signature files. (At events, advertise in local newspapers and on radio—event staff apparel also offers an opportunity to promote the website.)

5. Send email and "snail mail" press releases to announce your site. When you launch your site, add something or hold a special activity on your site, you can generate traffic through press coverage. Press releases are cheap, and they can produce stories in both electronic and traditional media. These stories send a temporary burst of visitors to you, and the leads are qualified because the respondents are interested in the topic of your release.

6. Swap or buy banner advertisements on other sites. As opposed to text links (#3, above), banner ads deliver short-term bursts of visitors to your site. That can be expensive, but there are services that swap banner space on your site in exchange for displaying your banners on other sites. Swapped banners usually generate less-qualified traffic than targeted banner ads, but they cost much less.

7. Pay commissions to affiliates who send customers to you. You may have noticed that some website have recommended reading lists, and when you click on the title, you are sent to a page selling that book on Amazon.com. This is no accident. If you buy the book from that page, Amazon pays a commission to the site that referred you. Those commissions have resulted in more than 50,000 sites selling millions of books for Amazon. Obviously, that method of driving traffic is suitable only if you, like Amazon, sell your products on the Web. An affiliate program of that sort is more complicated to set up than other traffic-driving methods, but it delivers the most rewarding visitors of all: paying customers. You don't pay for "click-through lookie-loos"; you pay only when somebody buys your product.

8. Carefully promote your site on newsgroups, chat lines, and email discussion lists. The key word here is *carefully.* Discussion groups can be worthwhile, but only if you move slowly and keep your eyes open. If you don't watch your step, this method can be the quickest way of alienating your prospects instead of attracting them. The reason is that on-line discussions tend to attract the people who are passionately interested in a topic. If you become a valued contributor to a discussion, not selling your products overtly but just answering questions, other participants may spread good electronic word-of-mouth about your company. This technique often translates into increased traffic on your website—and sales. Conversely, if you pepper on-line discussions with sales announcements, participants will get angry and drive traffic *away* from you.

9. Buy sponsorships of sites or pages that your prospects visit. Whereas banners are short-term traffic-drivers, sponsorships are long-term, suitable for driving ongoing traffic. You sponsor a page, an article or a section of a site for a specified time period, say a month or a year, perhaps longer. You usually pay per time period, regardless of how many visitors see the content that you sponsor. If you have chosen to sponsor content that's related to your prospects' needs, the response should be strong, and your site will be swamped with qualified visitors. Another benefit of sponsorship: It blocks competitors from running banners in your sponsored area.

Tip: **Don't spam your prospects!** All those email messages you receive promising "One million email addresses for $20!!!" and similar stuff fall into the spam category. If you buy or rent a list like this, beware. One marketer purchased 27 million addresses but, after removing duplicates, found that only 2.2 percent of them were actual addresses, and half of those were unusable. The names on such lists are not selected because they are interested in your product or service, so they are marginal prospects at best. The people have not asked to receive email, so many will be irritated by your message, and some may retaliate. If you want to grow your business by building relationships with repeat buyers, spam is not for you.

Technology is a palette; create with it

Using technology should be like selecting colors from an artist's palette. Never use some whiz-bang technology simply for the sake of trying to impress attendees. Occasionally the impulse to make the event visually stunning can result in multimedia overload. Just because you can, doesn't always mean that you should. Use technology to make a memorable connection. Use it to enhance your brand. Use it to connect the consumer to your brand. Use it to measure the effectiveness of your event. Sometimes the use of technology may be barely perceptible. Other times it may reinforce the notion that the medium is the message. The beauty of it is there for you to use in limitless ways. The only limitations are those you impose upon it.

Chapter Checklist

Checklist

- Event technology advances at light speed. Use it judiciously and don't get mired in it.

- The communications opportunities of the Internet have transformed how people get information about, register for, respond to, participate in and comment on events.

- Websites can contribute to an event's participatory dimension and extend its activities beyond the local event.

- Websites should be designed to be consistent with an event theme, they should be updated frequently and they should be capable of capturing as much useful data as possible.

Chapter 12
Measuring Event Marketing's Effectiveness

"Learning does not consist only of knowing what we must or we can do, but also of knowing what we could do and perhaps should not do."

— Umberto Eco, Italian semiologist

242

The Cosmic Spiderweb

There may have been a time when event marketing was seen as an adjunct to advertising, a subordinate element that might be nice to do but definitely something that could be absorbed by the advertising budget. However, that's no longer the case. Recent event research performed by Event Metrics Co. LLC® has pointed out that event marketing increases advertising awareness for a brand weeks and sometimes months after the event. As I've pointed out, event marketing has come of age, and part of the responsibility of maturity is accountability. These days, no marketing function gets a free ride. They all have to "justify their existence." It may sound harsh, but it makes good fiscal sense. After all, why would any company wish to continue to spend money to market its products with techniques and approaches that don't lead to sales of the products? That's a prescription for failure.

There are two basic reasons for measuring an event:

1. To determine how successfully your event met its objectives

2. To improve the effectiveness of subsequent event programs

No one way of measuring an event's success is the right way or even the only way. However, all measurement must be *actionable*. The key to effective measurement is to know going in what your objectives are and what the metrics are that will tell you whether you've met your objectives. This is what I call R.O.O. or "Return on Objectives." Some traditional methods of measurement include:

Attendance

If you have created enough buzz and have been diligent about announcing and promoting your event (a marquee act—appropriate to your product, of course—helps), and, if it's an outdoor event, the weather cooperates, you should be able to attract significant attendance. For most events, attendance is the indispensable factor for success. After all, if you don't get people into your event, you can't get them into a close, experiential relationship with your product, which is what it's all about. So, attendance is definitely important. It's also useful. You can make some assumptions based on attendance. For example, you can assume that those in attendance have an awareness of your product, unless they were asleep for the entire time.

Hand-raiser volumes

"Hand-raisers" are attendees who request additional information about your products. Demonstrations of interest like this indicate that attendees have gone beyond awareness to interest, so that hand-raiser volumes can measure how successful you've been in presenting your products. Of course, not everyone who is interested in your product will take the next step of requesting information, and some attendees collect information out of habit. Therefore, you have to be careful about the assumptions you make based on hand-raiser volumes. Nevertheless, any indication of interest on the prospective customer's part is an opportunity to move him or her further along the purchase funnel.

Consumer surveys

Unfortunately, raw attendance numbers and hand-raiser volumes cannot give you qualitative or quantitative data concerning attendees' attitudes and opinions about your product. You may be able to get a sense of their interest by noting how long they stay at the event, by how much enthusiasm they show, even by observing their facial expressions. But these impressions won't give you what you really need to know. Consumer surveys, which rely on verbal feedback (qualitative) from attendees, can go much further. Depending on what your objectives are for any given event, the consumer survey will elicit responses from attendees on issues of importance to you. Surveys can either be on-site (intercept surveys) or post-event, usually via phone. Event marketers often conduct both. Obviously, the on-site type of survey is a more immediate reflection of consumers' thoughts, although that doesn't necessarily make it more reliable. But while on-site, consumers are a "captive audience" and are probably less resentful about being asked questions than if they are phoned a few weeks later while they're sitting down to dinner.

How the interview questionnaire is developed is extremely important if the survey is to yield useful data. The old computer data input-output mantra applies here: "Garbage in, garbage out."

Another danger of consumer surveys is that marketers are often tempted to extrapolate the results to a larger universe of consumers. It is critical that this temptation be avoided. Consumer surveys are not "representative" of the market at-large. They simply reflect the moods and preferences of the people who attended the event.

Until recently, consumer surveys have proven to be laborious undertakings. Interviewers with clipboards (often these are college students working on a part-time, temporary basis) usually wandered around events, interrupting attendees (which establishes an uncomfortable relationship and lessens the "positively memorable" experience). Because there is usually no selection process for the sample of respondents beyond talking to whomever seems willing to spend a few minutes answering questions, an already unrepresentative group becomes even less representative (and the interviewers themselves can and do introduce dangerous biases into the process). And because you have fallible human beings conducting the interviews, the process is inevitably going to have errors. Even the best interviewers will occasionally skip a question, misunderstand an answer or check the wrong box. In addition, this manual process is time-consuming. As in the case of mall intercepts, interviewers might complete no more than two or three interviews *per hour*. If several interviewers are working the event, they may be lucky to get 100–150 people. Statistically, they have about an 80–85 percent confidence level, plus or minus seven percent. Not numbers to inspire confidence in your results.

However, new data collection technologies have begun to revolutionize this process. We'll take a look at an example a little further on.

But what if the clipboard-intercept survey approach is your only option?

For whatever reason—budget constraints, lack of technical capability, etc.—many event managers will find that the only way they can conduct on-site surveys is the old-fashioned, pseudo-mall-intercept way, the wandering clipboard-bearer who stops attendees to ask them questions about their experiences and opinions. If this is your only option, *Event Marketer Online* recommends adhering to the following eight steps for on-site surveys:

Step 1: Start with "soft questions" to get respondents comfortable and make them feel that they'll be able to handle the interview. "Was the parking convenient?" "Did you enjoy the halftime show?"

Step 2: Begin with unaided questions and help the participant if he or she starts to struggle. An example: Offer an unaided query ("Name as many sponsors of this event as you can"), then stop when the surveyee starts looking for signage. If the consumer can't name your brand, try a category-aided question ("Do you know of any soda sponsors of this event?") If they strike out again, hit them with the aided-awareness technique ("Are you aware that Brand X is a sponsor of this event?").

Step 3: Fire multiple-choice questions. "How does knowing X sponsors this event affect your opinion of the brand?" (Choices: Improves, Same, Decreases.) "How will X's involvement at this event change your purchase likelihood? (More, Same, Less Likely.) "How appropriate is it that X is associated with this event/sport/team?" (Very, Moderately, N/A).

Step 4: Move into open-ended questions about the brand. Example: "What do you think X is trying to say to you by sponsoring this event?"

Step 5: Next come open-ended questions about the event's activities, which are "heart of the survey" according to David Willis, CEO of Houston-based survey specialist Real Feedback, which handles on-site and telephone surveys for the likes of Toyota and Ford Motor Co. "Did you visit the brand's exhibit? What did you like? What didn't you like? Why do you think X is sponsoring this event? What is the benefit of X being here? What are some adjectives that you associate with X?"

Step 6: Serve up ownership questions about the sponsor's products. If the sponsor is a car company, ask what car they drive, when they last bought an automobile, what type of vehicle they'd buy today if they were buying, etc.

Step 7: Get the consumer's first name and ask if he or she would mind providing a phone number "for verification purposes" (80 percent will give up the digits, Willis says). Then end by asking if they'd be willing to participate in follow-up research (again, most agree) and thank them for their time.

Step 8: Follow up via phone or email with a section of the respondents to see if anything has changed. Ask the same questions and compare notes. (For an added bonus, do a random calling to consumers in the geographic area the night before the event starts.)

The numbers: On-site surveys cost between $10,000 and $18,000, depending on the window of opportunity, the sample size (should be at least 200) and the number of questions (remember, you must measure against actionable objectives). Off-site telephone efforts will run between $5,000 and $10,000 plus the cost of an incentive to spend time with the interviewer—depending on the quality and quantity of the lead list and the length of the survey (keep it under four minutes). This should allow for between 15 and 20 questions.

Recent telemarketing privacy laws and telephone privacy systems are making it increasingly difficult to "cold call" respondents. This will undoubtedly affect telephone-based research costs in the future as more calls will have to be made to reach statistical sample requirements.

What should be included in the survey questionnaire?

For most events, you want to get information from attendees in three major areas: demographics, event specifics and product specifics. Of the three, demographics is probably the least important, although it is useful data. And demographics becomes more important depending on how successfully you are able to "slice and dice" the information. Building a database should always be part of the event research objectives. For example, if you can identify household incomes in $10,000 increments rather than, say, $25,000 increments, you can learn more when it comes to what is called the multivariant analysis of the data. Without getting too technical in this context, suffice it to say that the more specific you can get in your profiles of customers, the better you can target your messages and event activities, not to mention identify potential buyers.

Of the remaining two information areas, the most important is (actionable) products specifics. The events specifics, after all, are easy enough to change. If you learn through your survey that a majority of attendees didn't like a specific activity, thought the lines were too long at the rest rooms or wanted changes to the food menu, these things can be addressed rather easily. Speed and analysis are also key. Get the answers in time to change any negative aspects and capitalize on the positive aspects. Answers related to your objectives should be available to you in a matter of hours and days ... not weeks and months.

Information on product specifics, however, can provide valuable insight into your target audience's buying habits and preferences. Product-specific questions might ask how far away customers are from purchasing a new car, for example, and what brand was their first choice. These questions can then be "cross-tabbed" with demographic data to reveal important trends. For example, you may learn that, although you've been targeting single females between the ages of 25 and 40 for a specific product, it's actually more popular among married people between the ages of 45 and 60.

Other questions of methodology

Putting together a questionnaire is an art in itself. Questions should be phrased in a way that eliminates as much bias as possible. The following example is very basic, but illustrates the point. A survey question is worded as follows: "When do you plan to buy a new vehicle?" Already, the question makes at least two assumptions that the survey should be *determining* rather than assuming—that the responder intends to buy his or her next vehicle (rather than leasing) and that he or she intends to buy a *new* vehicle, rather than a used, or "previously owned," vehicle, in the new vernacular. And what if the responder uses a company car? Again, it's an oversimplified example, but it demonstrates how a poorly constructed survey questionnaire can yield faulty or useless data.

The sequence of questions is also important. If the question above— "When do you plan to buy a new vehicle?"—is asked at the appropriate place in the survey, it becomes more relevant. In the classic "mall intercept" survey style, people are literally being interrupted and are often impatient to get the survey over with; this doesn't provide you with reliable learning. Attendees may not have had the opportunity to participate in the total event experience when they're "interrupted" by the surveyor. Keeping in mind that most survey questionnaires save the least important information—the demographic data—for the last questions, in case the interview gets cut short. This is the case with most telephone surveys as well.

Even physical location plays a part in bias. If the station where your data is being collected is in an area that captures respondents before they've had an opportunity to experience the entire event, this can obviously affect their opinions (which is why most such stations are located near exits). At Camp Jeep, Event Metrics Co.'s EchO™ program told us it was possible for respondents to have filled out the survey after taking test drives on the various courses. These test drives are exhilarating activities; many people would be so pumped after coming off the Rubicon Challenge Course, for example, that they might be ready to buy a Jeep Rubicon at that moment. Upon more sober reflection later at home, they might realize that in spite of their enthusiasm for the model and its performance, they aren't quite ready to buy a car. Nevertheless, if they fill out the questionnaire right after that ride, bias can be introduced into their answers. This is where interpretation of the data comes in and this is why

"The best event you've ever done is the one you haven't done yet."

It sounds paradoxical, but that's the way event marketers have to think. Once you become so enamored of your previous event achievements, you will have already lost ground to your competitors.  That's because of a number of reasons—the shorter attention span of today's consumer, the "clutter" of competitive events, the pressures to be on the cutting edge of popular culture. But mainly it has to do with the intrinsically dynamic nature of events themselves, how they tap into ever-changing emotions and experiences, neither of which, by definition, can have permanent "monuments" erected to them.

it's also helpful to have people who will be interpreting your data attend the event to understand these nuances. Another option is to take photos for this purpose. In either case, it is important that data be interpreted in *context.*

Media impressions

Media impressions include everything from paid advertising to news coverage of your event garnered through publicity. Depending on the size of the market where your event takes place, how much money you've spent in advertising and how hard your PR team has worked to generate publicity, this can be a big number. Unfortunately, it can also be a *misleading* number. It can give you a sense of how many people you have reached, but it can't tell you definitively how "reach" translates into preference or sales or even awareness. Since the compilation of media impressions doesn't typically provide feedback, it doesn't help you understand how to improve your event for the future. Nevertheless, if one of your event objectives was to increase your product's visibility, media impressions can be a useful metric, and, as such, it is one more tool in the measurement mix.

With regard to analyzing news coverage of your event, it is important not only to determine the *number* of "hits" (stories and mentions in print and electronic media) but also to assess the quality of the coverage. Was the coverage favorable? Did your key messages get mentioned? Did the stories show up in outlets that your target audiences were likely to see, and were the stories prominent (or buried where people would have to look for them)? All of these issues figure into the quality of news coverage and should be taken into account.

Incentive redemptions

If part of your event includes the distribution of, say, money-saving coupons as an incentive to or a reward for attending, the number of coupons redeemed can give you perhaps the ultimate feedback on how effective your event has been, since coupon redemptions mean sales.

Website hits

While it's not an entirely reliable measure of interest or awareness in your product or event (almost no form of measurement is *entirely* reliable or *actionable*), the tally of hits on your event website offers another facet of the overall measurement picture. The reason it's not totally reliable has to do with the nature of the Internet itself. Sometimes—often, as a matter of fact—where you land on the Internet is a matter of happenstance, as anyone who has ever surfed the Net will tell you. Hence, some of the hits will be accidental. On the other hand, a good percentage of them will be from people who navigated to your site because they had an interest in your event. One way of capturing information on those visitors to the site who are really interested in your event is to include a form on your website for people to request additional information.

Recent measurement technology

By replacing the traditional method of paper and pencil data collection, new electronic database systems are capable of event on-site and post-event surveying processes that can collect, sort, chart and report data with speed and accuracy within hours or days of the event. This technology enhances on-site survey and data capture, resulting in solid statistical metrics that assist the strategic planning process.

One such system, called EchO, developed by Michigan-based Event Metrics Company, LLC uses a proprietary method that actually quantifies the participant excitement and the power of word-of-mouth. The improved methodology and more accurate metrics (±3 percentage points at a 90 percent confidence level) encourage budget economies and enhance event strategies.

"The average paper questionnaire allows for maybe fifteen questions," says Grant Griffin, who heads up Event Metrics Company. "In the same amount of time, we can run them through fifty-two questions." The implications are significant, especially when you realize that the efficiencies of the EchO system (which utilizes proprietary software and electronic data generating stations in one location for both quantitative and qualitative entry by attendees), mean that the number of respondents can be greatly increased as well—doubled or even tripled. Thus, instead of getting maybe 100 respondents to answer 15 questions for a total of 1,500 data points, you now get perhaps 500 people to respond to 50+ questions for a number in excess of 25,000 data points per event. Obviously, the more data points you can collect, the richer the analysis will be on the back end. Always make "building the database" part of your strategic objective.

The process also allows for much greater flexibility. If a question needs to be added in the midst of an event, it can be programmed in to accommodate the next day's data collection. And then there's the issue of speed. Reports that used to take weeks to compile and develop now take a matter of hours. Imagine the opportunities gained from taking immediate action to positive consumer/attendee responses? The payoff is nearly just as immediate.

Most important, data collection methods like the EchO system offer an actionable relational database; a "value-based" system whereby information is organized so that its contents can be cross-referenced in hours instead of weeks. This helps companies match data points in interesting and creative ways that can yield significant insights into consumer habits and preferences.

The importance of sampling

The concept of sampling provides that the more representative your respondents are to the entire number of attendees at your event, the more confidence you can have in the data they provide through their answers. Never accept data with a statistical significance level of less than 90 percent confidence and a percentage "swing" of more than ±5 percent. Most public opinion survey experts would be wary of accepting anything less than an 85 percent level of this confidence. As I mentioned earlier, it is rarely possible to get this level of confidence through manual surveys of strolling interviewers who introduce biases into their sample. That isn't to say that you shouldn't do that kind of survey if that's all your budget will allow. You just need to understand that your data may be less reliable with a smaller sample.

Camp Jeep EchO™ facility—measurement program used for DaimlerChrysler brand events.

Numbers crunchers and strategists

There are numbers crunchers and there are strategists. A strategist takes what the numbers cruncher does and interprets it. The numbers crunchers—statisticians, that is—can tell you about the numbers' statistical significance, but that doesn't necessarily mean that they know what to do about it. Just because someone has a Ph.D. in statistics doesn't mean he or she understands your products or industry or has a sense of marketing. In other words, for your analysis, you need a professional who has a sense of the context for your survey results and your objectives, and who understands how the data can be applied to make the data/learning *actionable*.

Return on objectives (R.O.O. versus R.O.I.)

In the event marketing field, as in most marketing arenas, concern about return on investment has evolved into something close to an obsession. Essentially, return on investment refers to the "return" (incremental gain) from an action divided by the cost of that action. For example, if your event costs $200,000 and you expect to gain an additional $300,000 in sales as a result of the event, your return on investment calculation is ($300,000 − 200,000) / $200,000 = 50 percent. Sounds easy enough. Unfortunately, the calculation is never *that* easy. Other factors must be taken into consideration, such as profit margins and time frames (how far out will the event affect sales?).

Opinions on the ability to calculate return on investment for various marketing approaches vary. A number of intangibles exist. For example, your event might not be designed to generate sales directly. Does that mean it hasn't had any value? How do you measure customer goodwill and loyalty, after all? Because of these uncertainties, Event Metrics Company's Grant Griffin suggests that event managers would do well to ascertain how well their event meets *objectives*, as opposed to obsessing about return on investment. "Sales is not the only way to measure an event," he says. "Just because customers prefer your

256

brand doesn't mean that they are ready to buy today. So, will they go out and buy a new car or product right after attending your event? Only if you catch them at the point in the purchase cycle when they need a new car or product. To that extent, ROI is difficult to measure. But when they *do* decide to buy, whether it's tomorrow or two years down the road, you want to make sure that your brand is still their first preference. That means your objective is to have a positive experience of your brand, so that they will be inclined to purchase it when they're ready. And even though it's subjective, you can measure a positive experience. That's what return on objective is all about."

This is also why it is so important to clearly establish objectives for the event in advance. In the next chapter, which analyzes the Camp Jeep 2003 event, we'll look at how some of the data that was collected at the event was turned into immediately actionable knowledge that marketers can use.

Chapter Checklist

Checklist

- Event measurement should achieve two goals: 1) determining how successfully the event met its objectives and, 2) helping improve the effectiveness of subsequent events.

- Various measurement methods include:
    - Attendance
    - Hand raiser volumes
    - Consumer surveys
    - Media impressions
    - Incentive redemptions
    - Website hits

- New survey technology such as the EchO system can yield even more useful quantitative and qualitative data for marketers by increasing the number of surveys that can be conducted, increasing the data points and by cross-referencing relational database information. EchO also produces actionable results in hours and days instead of weeks and months after the event program has been completed.

Chapter 13

Case Study: Putting it All Together: The Camp Jeep Phenomenon

History

Camp Jeep, the annual owner-loyalty event for Jeep vehicle owners, was created in 1995 as an opportunity for Jeep enthusiasts to establish a bond with the Jeep brand and to form a sense of community with other consumers who shared their passion. Since its creation, Camp Jeep has become a benchmark among owner-loyalty events in the automotive industry and beyond.

The first Camp Jeep event in 1995 was modest by the standards of current-day Camp Jeep events, but the objectives have remained consistent for the decade-long history of the event. Those objectives are to:

- Build owner loyalty
- Strengthen the brand/owner bond
- Educate consumers on the off-road capability of Jeep vehicles
- Create an owner dialog with Jeep engineers
- Showcase the Jeep products

Main entrance at Camp Jeep 2003, Charlottesville, Virginia.

Although the scale of the 1995 event was smaller by today's standards, the concept was the same: provide off-road trail experiences, activities and entertainment all tying back to the Jeep brand and lifestyle. After that first year, it was apparent that Camp Jeep would grow, and for nine consecutive years (as of 2003), it has.

Camp Jeep has changed locations over the years as well, seeking venues that appeal to the lifestyle preferences of Jeep owners and can accommodate the growing popularity of the event. From 1995 through 1998, the event was held at Camp Hale in the Rocky Mountains of Colorado. In 1999, the event moved east for three years to Oak Ridge Estate in the Blue Ridge Mountains of Virginia. In 2002, the Camp Jeep traveled to the Midwest and the Bar W Ranch in the Ozark Mountains of Missouri. In 2003, it returned to Oak Ridge Estate in the Blue Ridge Mountains.

DaimlerChrysler continues to invest in Camp Jeep because it recognizes the value of continuing the bond between a customer and a brand. Few brands enjoy the customer loyalty of the Jeep brand. To ignore the intensity of

Lou with Julie Foudy, co-captain of the Olympic gold medal U.S. Women's Soccer Team, conducting soccer clinics for kids at Camp Jeep, Charlottesville, Virginia, 1999.

this loyalty among customers would not only be irresponsible and nonresponsive, it would be walking away from future sales. DaimlerChrysler has chosen, instead, to encourage and strengthen that bond through events like Camp Jeep. In order to keep the program fresh—and keep attendees coming back year after year—new activities and entertainment are produced for each year, frequently based on the input of attendees themselves.

Situation analysis

Every program that makes up part of the marketing mix for the Jeep brand requires a rationale for the money proposed to be spent on it. This applies to events as well. Whether it is an owner loyalty event or a sponsorship of a sporting event, it has to make sense for the brand. Each proposal and idea for an event is put through the same evaluation process to ensure an even comparison among all programs to be able to determine the best use of event marketing.

Events have the unique ability to target and invite a qualified audience. Events can provide customers a distinct engaging experience and can drive them to retail. Unlike many other disciplines, events can move attendees through the vehicle purchase funnel in consideration, shopping and, ultimately, to purchase, as has been demonstrated continually through measurement.

Camp Jeep provides Jeep owners the ultimate Jeep ownership experience with an emphasis on environment, education and entertainment—thereby building owner loyalty and equity in the Jeep brand. Jeep owners have a variety of lifestyle-affinity activities to choose from at Camp Jeep, such as the Thrills & Spills Zone, Jeep 101, 4x4 Trail Rides, Mountain Biking, Engineering Roundtables, Hiking, Kayaking, Outdoor Survival Skills, Fly Casting, Kids' Activities and Jeep Jubilee, which features a fireworks display and top-notch entertainment.

The following case study summarizes the key activities, facts and results of Camp Jeep 2003.

Case Study Report of Camp Jeep
Oak Ridge Estate
Blue Ridge Mountains, VA
June 26-28, 2003

Contents

Overview

Investment

Return

- Attendance
- Media impressions
- Sales

Creative

- Owner communications
- Advertising
- Website

Recommendations

- Observations for '04

Camp Jeep Mission Statement

To provide our Jeep owners and lessees a "peak experience" with an emphasis on the environment, education and entertainment.

Camp Jeep History

1995 –1998
- Vail, Colorado
- Camp Hale in the Rocky Mountains

1999 – 2001
- Charlottesville, Virginia
- Oak Ridge Estate in the Blue Ridge Mountains

2002
- Branson, Missouri
- Bar W Ranch in the Ozark Mountains

2003
- Charlottesville, Virginia
- Oak Ridge Estate in the Blue Ridge Mountains

Camp Jeep 2003 Details

- Event dates: June 26-28, 2003

- Location: Oak Ridge Estate (near Charlottesville, VA)

- Blue Ridge Mountains

- Cost: $325 per Jeep vehicle

- Invitees: Exclusively Jeep owners and their guests invited for all three days

- Entertainment: Smash Mouth

Camp Jeep 2003 Facts

- Over 2,000 vehicles registered; 10,000 people attended.

- Jeep owners from 46 states were represented.

- 1,400 people drove the new Tomb Raider edition Wrangler Rubicon on the Rubicon Challenge Course.

- 3,390 4x4 trail rides were scheduled over the three days..

- 6,000 people drove the Jeep 101 courses.

- Twice as many Liberty owners attended Camp Jeep compared to last year.

- 1,200 Jeep owners went kayaking.

Camp Jeep 2003 Facts :

- CMT, *Detroit Free Press*, WJR, *Motor Trend* and *4-Wheeler* all were in attendance.

- Non-paid media value of over $15 million.

- In 2001, 6.4% of registered owners bought new vehicles (from NVDR).

- Won Best Activity Generating Brand Loyalty at PRO Awards 2002.

- Won Best Activity Generating Brand Loyalty at the APMA Worldwide Awards.

- Finalist for Best Global Event in 2002.

Camp Jeep 2003 Activities

- 4x4 Trail Rides
- Jeep 101 Courses
- Engineering Roundtables
- Jeep Museum
- Rubicon Challenge Course
- Hiking
- Kayaking
- Adventure Tower
- Fly Casting
- Kids' Activities
- Thrills & Spills Zone
- Scuba Diving
- Outdoor Grilling Lessons
- Outdoor Survival Classes

Camp Jeep 2003 Villages

Jeep 101 Village
- 101 courses
- Mopar

World of Jeep Village
- Provisions Store
- Jeep Museum

Engineering Village
- Engineering Roundtables
- Engineering Tech Center

Kids' Village
- Crafts, games, etc.
- Mini Jeep 101 Course

Adventure Village
- Adventure Tower
- Outdoor Grilling Classes
- Kayaking

Camp Jeep Café Village
- Food and beverages

Sports Village
- Thrills & Spills Zone
- Fly Casting

Tomb Raider Village
- Rubicon Challenge Course
- Remote Control Jeep 101 course

Camp Jeep 2003 Villages

Jeep 101 Village consisted of two Jeep 101 courses—
Jeep Agility and Reverse Steer—Mopar Store and
"The Way Out" Polaris Experience.

- A total 2,228 drivers went through the courses over
the three days.

- There were 3,824 total experiences on the Jeep 101
course.

- Over 800 demo rides were conducted on the 11 different Polaris vehicles that were on the course.

- Mopar installed over 150 accessories on-site and
doubled the maintenance product sales this year.

Camp Jeep 2003 Villages:

Engineering Village

- Engineering Technology Center

    - Owners spoke one-on-one with Jeep engineers and automotive suppliers.
    - Five OEM suppliers participated in 2003.
    - Tech Center includes "Ask An Engineer" area.

- Engineering Roundtables

    - 75-minute sessions geared for owners to ask questions about their Jeep vehicle.
    - Approximately 900 owners participated.

- High Mileage Wrangler Inspection

    - Engineers wanted to learn more about Wrangler vehicles that had high mileage.
    - 50 vehicles were inspected.

Camp Jeep 2003 Villages:

Camp Kids Village

- Nine Arts & Crafts activities, including Flip Flop Decorating and Bird Houses, were available.

- Nine activities made up Fun & Games, such as Make Your Own Music Video and Mini Jeep 101.

- A variety of presentations were attended at the Kids' Stage, including:
  - Hip Hop Dance Lessons
  - Folk Songs
  - Boy Scouts Camp Skills
  - Virginia Museum of Natural History Workshops

Camp Jeep 2003 Villages:

Adventure Village activities included the Adventure Tower, Kayaking, Hiking, Speaker Presentations, the Coleman Grilling School, Climb-ing Wall, and many others

- A total of 1,600 Camp Jeep attendees of all ages braved the Adventure Tower.

- The Coleman Grilling School educated 1,500 Camp Jeep guests over the three days.

- Over 700 songs were sung and recorded in the Karaoke Tent.

- 350 kites were flown over the rolling hillside of Camp Jeep.

- Numerous autographs were given by famed *National Geographic* photographer Sam Abell in the Grand Cherokee Blacked Out Tent.

Camp Jeep 2003 Villages:

Sports Village once again contained the popular Thrills & Spills Zone, as well as Fly Casting, Paintball, and the Scuba Tank.

- All of the activities that young children could participate in sold out the quickest, and the instructors were willing to teach children of any age.

- Fly Casting sessions sold out every day, accommodating more than 600 people over the three days.

- The Scuba Tank was very popular. Due to extreme heat of Virginia, 926 Camp Jeep attendees took a lesson in the pool.

Camp Jeep 2003 Villages

Tomb Raider Village

- Rubicon Challenge Course

    - 1,400 Jeeps drove the *Tomb Raider*-themed Rubicon Challenge Course, complete with moguls, logs and and a rock hill.

- Paramount Cave

    - Paramount sponsored the *Lara Croft Tomb Raider: Cradle of Life Mobile Cave,* which gave owners a sneak peak at the trailer, costumes and other fun facts from the movie.

- Remote Control Jeep Course

    - 2,006 owners drove a remote-control Jeep model through a challenging obstacle course.

    - Owners discussed various aspects of the hobby of radio-controlled modeling.

- Esquire Tent

    - Keepsake photographs were taken of the owners at the finish line of the Rubicon Challenge Course.

Emerging Artist Concert:

Thursday night featured emerging acts such as Josh Kelly, Alice Peacock, Justincase and The Rising. The concert was held at the same location as the Jeep Jubilee on Saturday.

Josh Kelly

The Rising

Alice Peacock

Saturday Night Jeep Jubilee

- Saturday night ended with an incredible performance by Smash Mouth and a spectacular fireworks display.

- Over 8,000 picnic dinners were served.

Camp Jeep Partners

- Camp Jeep 2003 created a cross-marketing platform with several brand partners in mind.

- Partners were able to utilize Camp Jeep as an opportunity to seed a relationship with the wildly popular Jeep brand and defined lifestyle.

- Over $540,000 in "added value" was brought to Camp Jeep through several partners.

Lou Bitonti

Camp Jeep Results — Statistics and Media

- In 2003, Camp Jeep saw over 2,000 Jeep owners register for the annual three-day event.

- Close to 10,000 people were on-site at the Oak Ridge Estate for Camp Jeep 2003.

- Over $540,000 in "added value" was brought to Camp Jeep through several partners.

- The non-paid media value, to date, for Camp Jeep is approximately $15 million.

- Attending media included representation from Los Angeles, New York, Pittsburgh, Detroit, Baltimore and as far away as Spain.

- The following media outlets/journalists attended Camp Jeep 2003:
  - –WJR 760 AM
  - –MotorWeek TV
  - –CMT (Country Music Television)
  - –*The Detroit News*
  - –Petersen's *4-Wheel and Off Road* magazines
  - –*PopStar* magazine
  - –*Ediaction News* (Spanish automotive publication)
  - –Lynne Margolis (music industry freelance writer)
  - –Evelynn Kanter (business/feature freelance writer)

  Live on-site radio remotes included:

Thursday, June 26

  –WCYK 99.7 FM (country format) – 4 hours live on-site

Saturday, June 28

  –WJR 760 AM – 3 hours live on-site
  –WUMX 107.5 FM (lite-rock format) – 3 hours live on-site

Camp Jeep Results — Media

Local and regional attending media included the following:

- WDBJ (CBS), Lynchburg
- WSET (ABC), Lynchburg
- WVIR (NBC), Charlottesville
- *Charlottesville Daily Progress*
- *Hopewell News*
- *The News and Advance*
- *The News Virginian*
- *The Waynesboro News*

Pre-event coverage included:

- A national radio tour with approximately 28 radio interviews
- *Advertising Age*
- *Automotive News*
- *Chicago Tribune*
- *Money Magazine*
- *Parade Magazine*

Camp Jeep Results — Sales

- A sales sweep from Camp Jeep 2003 attendees will be performed in late August and again in December to allow for sales to be realized.

- In 2002, 7% of registered Camp Jeep attendees bought new Jeep vehicles.

- In 2001, 6.4% of registered Camp Jeep attendees bought new Jeep vehicles.

Camp Jeep Creative Elements

Direct Mail—A series of communications was sent out to Jeep owners to invite and educate them about Camp Jeep.

"Save the Date" Postcard – 29,000 pieces sent out

Direct Mail Invitation—
350,000 pieces sent out

Activity Sign-up Pack

Information Pack

Camp Jeep Creative Elements

Camp Jeep 2003 received substantial exposure in existing owner communication pieces.

The Jeep owner magazine

The dealer advantage brochure

Camp Jeep Creative Elements

- Camp Jeep-specific ads ran in off-roading enthusiast publications, such as the *UFWDA's Voice*.

- A mobile outdoor billboard was also strategically utilized in Virginia to increase event awareness.

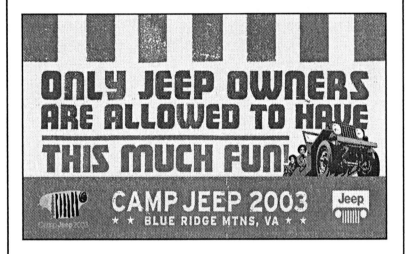

Camp Jeep Creative Elements

- More than half of Camp Jeep 2003's registrations came from the website

- 125,032 total visits took place through June.

- Most visitors were self-directed to the site.

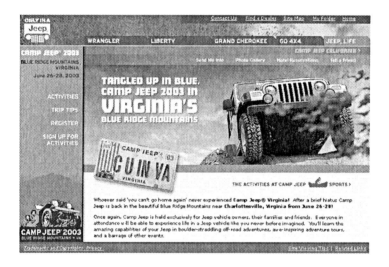

Camp Jeep After-action Report

Site Layout

- Bring back Expressions Village.

- Revisit placement of speakers and overall site sound.

- Addition of a lake at Oak Ridge would allow on-site water activities such as kayaking, fly casting and Polaris water crafts.

- All bleachers should have canopy covers to protect owners and children from the sun.

Engineering Village

- Increase the number of sessions for Engineering Roundtables to meet growing demand of attendees.

- Investigate an alternative location (i.e. quiet zone) for Engineering Roundtables, to help avoid complaints regarding noise levels.

- Expand the village just beyond the Engineering Tent and Roundtable sessions.

Camp Jeep After-action Report

Camp Jeep Café

- Increase menu options with more vegetarian and health-conscious selections.

- Cold sandwiches are an essential menu item.

- Consider utilizing Sirius trailer/stage as a separate daytime pavilion where owners can listen to live music throughout the course of the day.

Camp Kids' Village

- Due to excessive heat for children, investigate moving the Kids' Stage inside the larger air-conditioned tent.

- Close proximity to the Sirius stage presented some excessive noise problems.

- Post a "Parental Supervision Required" sign at the entrance of the Kids' Tent.

Camp Jeep After-action Report

World of Jeep Village

- Jeep Provisions (Gear) Store should investigate a new layout and display for store.

- The Jeep Museum should be a focus of the '04 event, including a historical evolution of the Wagoneer.

- Museum could feature different wings for different eras, focusing on the future of Jeep vehicles.

Jeep 101 Village

- Product Specialists conducting the walk-arounds should have full-line product catalogs to distribute on-site.

- Continue to keep the Rubicon Challenge Course toward the back of the site, which contributes to owners in line being less visible.

- Build a second Rubicon Challenge Course on-site.

- Investigate doing preregistration for course or flag system to help reduce lines.

Camp Jeep After-action Report

4x4 Trails

- Pre-egistration and on-site registration processes need to be revisited for better efficiency.

- Utilizing three separate tents for the 4x4 trail sign-ups would help alleviate some of the lines that formed Thursday morning.

- Moving these tents away from the front entrance will reduce the chances of any future bottlenecks.

Adventure Village

- More zip lines should be added to the Adventure Tower.

- The low ropes course of the Adventure Tower should be used as a qualifier for all participants to help reduce traffic flow problems.

- Multiple climbing walls with different degrees of difficulty could increase throughput next year.

Camp Jeep After-action Report

Sports Village

- Addition of a lake on-site would be a tremendous enhancement to the fly casting activity.

- Past activities such as Flight School and Archery should strongly be considered for a return in 2004.

- Overall size of Thrills & Spills should be increased.

- Skateboarding street course created in 2002 worked better than just the verticle ramp, which was not as conducive to participation.

Camp Jeep After-action Report

Entertainment

- A "name act" for all concerts is essential.

- Consider bringing back artists from previous Camp Jeep events (i.e. Sheryl Crow, Kenny Loggins, Blues Brothers) in celebration of the 10th Anniversary.

Owner Communications

- Include Camp Jeep video on an interactive CD-ROM direct mail invitation, which would then drive owners to the Jeep website.

- Consider including Trip Tips in the owner's gift bag, so as not to delay the mailing of the Final Event Kit.

- Allow for even greater sponsor exposure in all direct mail communications for maximum exposure and return.

Camp Jeep After-action Report

Miscellaneous

- Work with local counties to bring in more fun, interactive opening ceremonies.

- Additional cellular towers from more service providers would be a welcome addition in the area.

- Site walkthrough with clients should be at 9:00 am Wednesday morning.

"It's like an amusement park, an adventure camp and a Jeep museum all rolled into one."

On-site EchO Top Line Report

"Gems" From — Camp Jeep, Nelson County, Virginia

- 77% stated that their OPINION of Jeep was improved!

- 79% stated that their CONSIDERATION level of Jeep was improved!

- 89% stated that their PURCHASE INTENTION was raised!

- 84% stated that they would attend Camp Jeep AGAIN!

- 81% stated that Camp Jeep was "somewhat" or "very" SATISFYING!

- 88% stated that they would "RECOMMEND Camp Jeep to their "best friend."

Event: Camp Jeep 2003
Date: June 26-28, 2003
Location: Nelson County, Virginia
Factors: Weather: Friday, Saturday hot, humid, dusty; rain threat never happened.
Friday: Sunny, hot, humid, highs in the mid-90s
Saturday: Pleasant, overcast, highs in the low 80s
Sample Total: 641   Target Sample: 250

Return on Marketing Experience

- Camp Jeep made a big impact:

  —81% of participants rated the event "Somewhat" or "Very" Satisfying!

- Beyond The BUZZ—88% of participants state they would recommend the event to their "best friend."

  —Moreover, 84% would attend Camp Jeep again.

- 77% of participants stated that the Camp Jeep event improved their OPINION of Jeep!

- 79% of participants stated that the Camp Jeep event improved their CONSIDERATION of Jeep!

- 89% of participants reported that the Camp Jeep event had a positive impact on PURCHASE INTENTION!

Intended Purchase Profile

- 81% of attendees intend to purchase a new (not used) vehicle.

  —Compare to national average of 50%!

  —Highest intended segment for new purchase is Sport Utility Vehicle (62%), distantly followed by Car at 11%.

- They're In-market .

  — 26% of the respondents intend to purchase/lease in the next six months

  —15% in the 7-12 month area and just over 25% are in the 13-24 month time frame.

  —35% are at least two years away from purchase.

- Of those who intend to purchase a new vehicle, Wrangler Rubicon rates at the top with 27%, followed by Grand Cherokee (19%) Liberty (10%) and Wrangler (7%).

- Top-rated replacement vehicles (among those intending to buy a new vehicle) are:

  —Wrangler (17%), Grand Cherokee (17%), Liberty (6%) and Cherokee (6%).

- Top Garage Mates at the event are: Wrangler (20%), Grand Cherokee (11%), Cherokee (8%) and Liberty (6%).

Demographic Profiles — Who Came to Camp Jeep?

- 51% male, 49% female.

- 58% live in dual income households.

- Age distribution: 73% are 45 years old or younger.

- Household income (among all respondents) is very solid; 64% earn $50-120K.

  —82% earn more than $50K (the minimal threshold for a new vehicle purchase).

- Ethnicity: White/Caucasians comprise 95%.

- 65% are in married households.

- 80% live in suburbs or small towns/rural communities.

Education Level Is Strong

- 59% are college grads or have post-grad experience.

- Internet use among attendees is high: 96% (CRM contacts)

  —Time on-line is moderate; 56% spend only 2-10 hours/week on-line.

  —They'd probably rather be in their Jeeps than on-line.

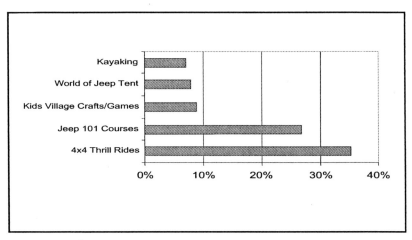

Passion Profile

- A pattern emerges among Camp Jeep participants for off-roading, camping trips, adventure vacations, travel (US), canoeing/rafting, driving for fun, hiking, mountain biking:

  —These are adventurous people who actively want to immerse themselves in the greater "out there"; their Jeep is the portal to that world.

- Leverage future Camp Jeep co-sponsorship and tie-in opportunities among these passions:

Off-Roading (4x4)	7.59%
Camping Trips	6.27%
Adventure Vacations	5.30%
Travel - US	4.24%
Canoeing/Rafting	3.86%
Driving for Fun	3.15%
Hiking	2.93%
Biking - Mountain	2.60%

Lou Bitonti

Additional:

Event Advertising:

32% "heard" about the Camp Jeep through invitations.

24% through the Internet.

17% through magazines.

Lou's Library

I've listed books that I have read and studied over the years. Many relate to the field of marketing and its ever-changing business environment. The content of these books illustrates many different subjects and points of view. You may agree or disagree with their positions.

But that's okay. The key to being a successful event manager is being open to the differences. You must continue throughout your career to nurture your curiosity. Keep feeding it with different points of view. You must continue to be a student of your craft, keep your unquenchable thirst for knowledge long after you're done with your academic training. It's the only way to stay fresh and survive in this world.

My "Hero List" is just my way of classifying certain personalities in business and society that I admire for various reasons. It's an eclectic list that doesn't necessarily conform to themes or categories. Primarily, the subjects or authors of these books are visionaries, but most importantly, they strove to make a difference in their life endeavors. Call them overachievers, self-centered, or in the right place at the right time. They took hold of me in the way Don Quixote seized life.

Since childhood, one of my great fears was that, one day, I might reflect on my life and discover that I had not made a difference. Maybe that's why coaching has a strong influence in my life. One never knows when a gesture or word of encouragement or a suggestion will make a difference in a fellow human being's view of life.

I have seen in my business career and in my personal and coaching world that I can generate enthusiasm and establish a sense of being part of a team. A team of athletes or a team of business professionals must focus on a mission statement and keep it the standard above everything else that can influence one's decision. To truly motivate your team, you must be dependable and responsible. I'll close with the following quote from the poet Edward Everett Hale:

> *I am only one,*
> *But still I am one.*
> *I cannot do everything*
> *But still I can do something;*
> *And because I cannot do everything*
> *I will not refuse to do the something that I can do.*

Marketing and General Business Books

Aaker, David A. and Erich Joachimsthaler. *Brand Leadership: Building Assets in an Information Economy.* New York: The Free Press, 2000.

Benn, Alec. *The 27 Most Common Mistakes in Advertising.* New York: AMACOM, 1981.

Bing, Stanley. *Throwing the Elephant: Zen and the Art of Managing Up.* New York: HarperCollins, 2002.

Blanchard, Ken, John P. Carlos and Alan Randolph. *Empowerment Takes More Than a Minute.* San Francisco: Berrett-Koehler, 1996.

Bond, Jonathan and Richard Kirshenbaum. *Under the Radar: Talking to Today's Cynical Consumer.* New York: John Wiley & Sons, 1997.

Caponigro, Jeffrey R. *The Crisis Counselor: A Step-by-Step Guide to Managing a Business Crisis.* Chicago: Contemporary Books, 2000.

Collins, James C. and Jerry I. Porras. *Built to Last: Successful Habits of Visionary Companies.* New York: HarperBusiness, 1994.

Cross, Richard and Janet Smith. *Customer Bonding: Pathway to Lasting Customer Loyalty.* New York: McGraw-Hill/Contemporary Books, 1996.

Della Femina, Jerry. *From Those Wonderful Folks Who Gave You Pearl Harbor.* New York: Simon & Schuster, 1970.

Dychtwald, Ken and Joe Flower. *Age Wave: The Challenges and Opportunities of an Aging America.* Los Angeles: J. P. Tarcher, 1989.

Gladwell, Malcolm. *The Tipping Point: How Little Things Can Make a Big Difference.* New York: Little, Brown and Company, 2000.

Gobé, Marc. *Emotional Branding: he New Paradigm for Connecting Brands to People.* New York: Allworth Press, 2001.

Godin, Seth. *Free Prize Inside! The Next Big Marketing Idea.* New York: Portfolio (The Penguin Group), 2004

Grove, Andrew S. *Only the Paranoid Survive: How to Exploit the Crisis Points that Challenge Every Company and Career.* New York: Doubleday, 1999.

Hall, Doug. *Jump Start Your Brain.* New York: Warner Books, 1996.

Hall, Doug with David Wecker. *The Maverick Mindset: Finding the Courage to Journey from Fear to Freedom.* New York: Simon & Schuster, 1997.

Hammer, Michael. *Beyond Reengineering: How the Process-Centered Organization Is Changing Our Work and Our Lives.* New York: HarperBusiness, 1997

Hendricks, Gay and Kate Ludeman. *The Corporate Mystic: A Guidebook for Visionaries with Their Feet on the Ground.* New York: Bantam Books, 1997.

Levin, Doron P. *Behind the Wheel at Chrysler: he Iacocca Legacy.* New York:Harcourt, 1995.

Levine, Michael. *Guerrilla P.R.: How You Can Wage an Effective Publicity Campaign . . . Without Going Broke.* New York: HarperBusiness, 1994.

Lois, George with Bill Pitts. George, *Be Careful: A Greek Florist's Kid in the Roughhouse World of Advertising.* New York: Saturday Review Press, 1972.

Maxwell, John C. *The 17 Essential Qualities of a Team Player: Becoming the Kind of Person Every Team Wants.* Nashville: Thomas Nelson, 2002.

Maxwell, John C. *The 21 Irrefutable Laws of Leadership.* Nashville: ThomasNelson, 1998.

McCormack, Mark H. *What They Don't Teach You at Harvard Business School.* New York: Bantam Books, 1988.

Meyer, Paul and Randy Slechta. *The 5 Pillars of Leadership: How to Bridge the Leadership Gap.* Tulsa, OK: Insight Publishing Group, 2002.

Moritz, Michael and Barrett Seaman. *Going for Broke: Lee Iacocca's Battle to Save Chrysler.* New York: Doubleday, 1981.

Myers, James H. *Segmentation and Positioning for Strategic Marketing Decisions.* Chicago: American Marketing Association, 1996.

Peppers, Don and Martha Rogers. *The One to One Future:Building Relationships One Customer at a Time*. New York: Doubleday, 1997.

Peters, Thomas and Robert H. Waterman, Jr. *In Search of Excellence: Lessons from America's Best-Run Companies*. New York: Warner Books, 1988.

Peters, Thomas. *Thriving on Chaos: Handbook for a Management Revolution*. New York: Alfred A. Knopf, 1991.

Pine II, Joseph B. and James H. Gilmore. *The Experience Economy: Work is Theatre & Every Business a Stage*. Boston: Harvard Business SchoolPress, 1999.

Raphel, Murray and Neil Raphel. *Up the Loyalty Ladder: Turning Sometime Customers into Full-time Advocates for Your Business*. Atlantic City: Raphel Marketing, 1995.

Ries, Al and Laura Ries. *The Fall of Advertising and the Rise of PR*. New York: HarperCollins, 2002.

Ries, Al and Jack Trout. *Marketing Warfare*. New York: McGraw/Hill, 1997.

Rosen, Emanuel. *The Anatomy of Buzz: How to Create Word-of-Mouth Marketing*. New York: Doubleday, 2002.

Schmitt, Bernd H. *Experiential Marketing: How to Get Customers to Sense/Feel/Think/Act/Relate to Your Company and Brands*. New York: The Free Press, 1999.

Shostrom, Everett L. *Man, the Manipulator: The Inner Journey from Manipulation to Actualization*. New York: Bantam Books, 1980.

Smith, J. Walker and Ann Clurman. *Rocking the Ages: The Yankelovich Report on Generational Marketing*. New York: HarperBusiness, 1997.

Spendolini, Michael J. *The Benchmarking Book*. New York: AMACOM, 1992.

Stanley, Thomas J. and William D. Danko. *The Millionaire Next Door: The Surprising Secrets of America's Wealth*. Atlanta: Longstreet Press, 1998.

Vlasic, Bill and Bradley A. Stertz. *Taken for a Ride: How Daimler-Benz Drove Off with Chrysler*. New York: HarperBusiness, 2001.

Weiss, Michael J. *The Clustering of America*. New York: Harper & Row (a TildenPress book), 1988.

Woolf, Brian P. *Customer Specific Marketing: The New Power in Retailing*. *Atlantic City*: Raphel Marketing, 1996.

Zyman, Sergio. *The End of Marketing as We Know It*. New York: HarperBusiness, 2000.

Lou's Hero Reading List

Gates, Bill. *Business @ the Speed of Thought: Succeeding in the Digital Economy*. New York: Warner Books, 2000.

Gelb, Arthur, Ed. *The New York Times Great Lives of the Twentieth Century*. BDD Promotional Book Co., 1988.

Iacocca, Lee with Sonny Kleinfeld. *Talking Straight*. New York: BantamDoubleday Dell, 1990.

Iacocca, Lee with William Novak. *Iacocca: An Autobiography*. New York: Bantam Books, 1986.

Kelley, Kitty. *His Way: The Unauthorized Biography of Frank Sinatra*. New York: Bantam Books, 1987.

Krames, Jeffrey A. *The Jack Welch Lexicon of Leadership: Over 250 Terms, Concepts, Strategies & Initiatives of the Legendary Leader*. New York: McGraw-Hill Trade, 2001.

Machiavelli, Niccolò. *The Prince*. New York: W.W. Norton, 1992.

Powell, Colin with Joseph E. Persico. *My American Journey*. New York: Random House, 1999.

Truman, Harry S. *Memoirs of Harry S. Truman*. New York: Doubleday, 1955.

Yeager, Chuck and Leo Janos. Yeager: *An Autobiography*. New York: Doubleday Dell Pub, 1985.

Zehme, Bill. *The Way You Wear Your Hat: Frank Sinatra and the Lost Art of Livin'*. New York: HarperCollins, 1997.

Index

LouDog Enterprises is a full-service event marketing consulting organization whose team of experts has more than 50 years of experience and an elite portfolio of event marketing successes to its credit.

If you would like more information on how our core team approach can help you create, evaluate, implement and measure an event to generate sales for your company, please call us tollfree at 1-866-334-5904 or visit the LouDog website at www.loudogenterprises.com.

If you enjoyed *The Cosmic Spiderweb*, please watch for the next book from Dog Eat Dog Publications:

Hidden Agendas: How to Survive in the Corporate World.

Hidden Agendas will look at what really motivates people in the business environment and how to understand the subtexts, codes, doublespeak and other duplicities that are a part of everyday corporate life from the mailroom to the boardroom.

We invite you to submit your favorite *Hidden Agenda* story. Please visit the *Hidden Agendas* website (www.hiddenagendas.net) for more information.

Printed in the United States
27925LVS00002B/1-42